Encyclopedia of Fashion Details

Patrick John Ireland

Encyclopedia of Fashion Details

B T Batsford Limited London

Phototypeset by Tek-Art Ltd, Kent
and printed in Great Britain by
Butler & Tanner Ltd
Frome, Somerset
for the publishers
B T Batsford Ltd
4 Fitzhardinge Street
London W1H 0AH

ISBN 0 7134 6433 X (limp)

Contents

Acknowledgment

The author would like to thank the students and staffs of the many colleges and workshops he has visited throughout the country who have inspired and encouraged him to compile this book, in particular the staff of the Library of the London College of Fashion for their ready help in aiding his research, also Joan Bale from Chelmsford Adult Education and Thelma Nye, my editor at Batsford, for her help, encourage-ment and patience in the preparation of this book.

The author and publisher acknowledge with thanks the following who have so willingly supplied photographs for inclusion in this volume: Anthea Godfrey, Design Department (Embroidery), London College of Fashion, and her students Sally Bannister pages 24, 91, Jean Bichara page 165, Maureen Briggs page 168, Mary Chandler pages 24, 165, Marina Constantinou pages 93, 95, 118, Kate Davis page 168, Angela Harrington page 167, Ethel Hewitt page 198, Joyce Hill pages 198, 204, Helen McGrail page 95, Catherine Pope pages 24, 95, Val Porter pages 125, 198, Delia Pusey pages 95, 167, Lyn Simons pages 118, 125; and Sara Woods page 167.

Heide Jenkins, part-time lecturer in embroidery at the London College of Fashion, page 157.

Courtaulds, Jaeger, Susan Small, Peggy Page, Du Pont Company (UK), Windsmoor (London) for montage on page 67.

J & P Coats for two top photographs on page 204

Jane West for the photographs of belts designed by Caroline Darke for Skimp Accessories pages 27-33.

Introduction

Planned as a reference for students, it is hoped that this book will be of equal value to the many people who are interested in fashion design.

Arranged in alphabetical order the contents illustrate fashion details and suggesting some of the many ways in which they may be used.

Techniques

Throughout the book the drawings vary from line diagrams showing the development of the use of a design detail to a variety of fashion sketches using line and tone values to show textures and patterns, and the way in which to indicate the drape and fall of materials; as well as describing how these graphic effects may be achieved.

Figure grids are provided for those who may have difficulties in sketching the human figure, especially during their early stages of study.

Design courses

When working on a design course the student will be required to produce sheets of design sketches when developing ideas. Working drawings and diagrammatic sketches are required for the sample room when cutting the pattern and making a garment. Presentation drawings are needed for exhibitions, competitions and assessments of work.

Students often work from design briefs which are set by the lecturers or manufacturers.

Photographs

Photographs have been used to illustrate the specific decorative effects of embroidery and as examples of different design techniques.

Drawing for examinations

When answering questions for certain examination papers a sketch or clear diagrammatic drawing is often required, combined with a description of a specific design or detail, ie collars, sleeves, pockets, yokes, etc. The methods illustrated are designed to help the student to cover this requirement.

Reference

These pages are presented for use as a reference to fashion details and decorative effects when designing. They illustrate some of the many ways in which style features, such as tucks, pleats, piping, pockets and collars, may be used in the design of a garment.

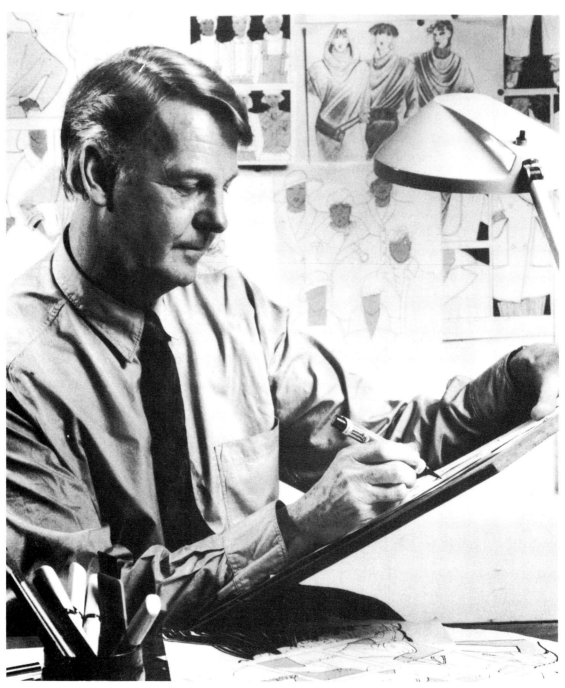

Patrick John Ireland.
Photograph by Derek Seddon

Figure drawing

This section is included to help those who may have difficulty, especially in the early stages, in drawing the human figure.

It would be an advantage to attend life-drawing classes and to make a study of anatomy but should this not be possible a figure template can be a useful guide for sketching and developing design ideas. A number of poses are illustrated here.

The average proportions of the figure are 7 1/2 to 8 heads to the body. Often fashion sketches are stylized and exaggerated when used for presentation and promotion purposes in order to emphasize a fashion image. But when sketching and developing design ideas it is usual to keep the sketches to the average proportions without too much exaggeration, enabling the shape, cut and general design details which relate to the figure to be clearly seen, giving attention to the placing of the collar, pockets, buttons, etc.

The fashion image suggested is important. This may be projected through the sketch by selecting a suitable pose for the design, ie sporty/casual, elegant/ sophisticated.

The face and hair styles need only be suggested but should project the image suitable to the design.

Throughout the book a selection of figures has been illustrated using different techniques and simple descriptions of the media used have been given. The drawing techniques vary from like diagrams to free-style sketches.

Figure drawing

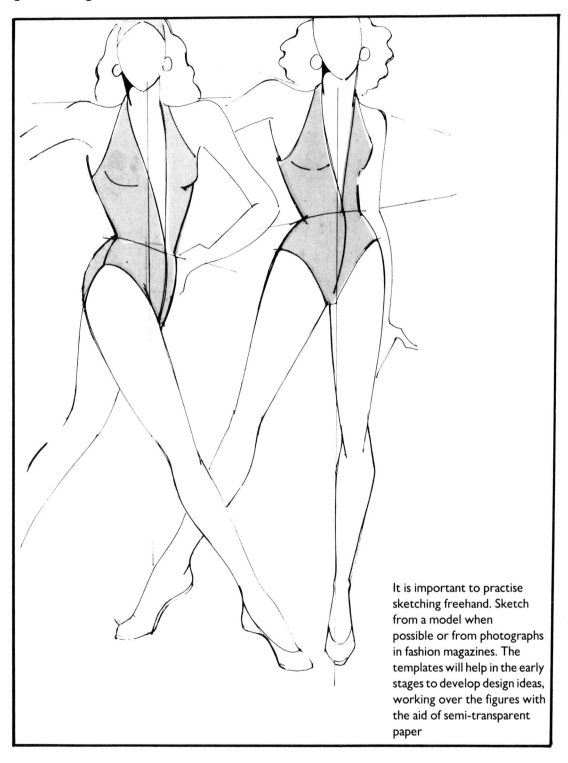

It is important to practise sketching freehand. Sketch from a model when possible or from photographs in fashion magazines. The templates will help in the early stages to develop design ideas, working over the figures with the aid of semi-transparent paper

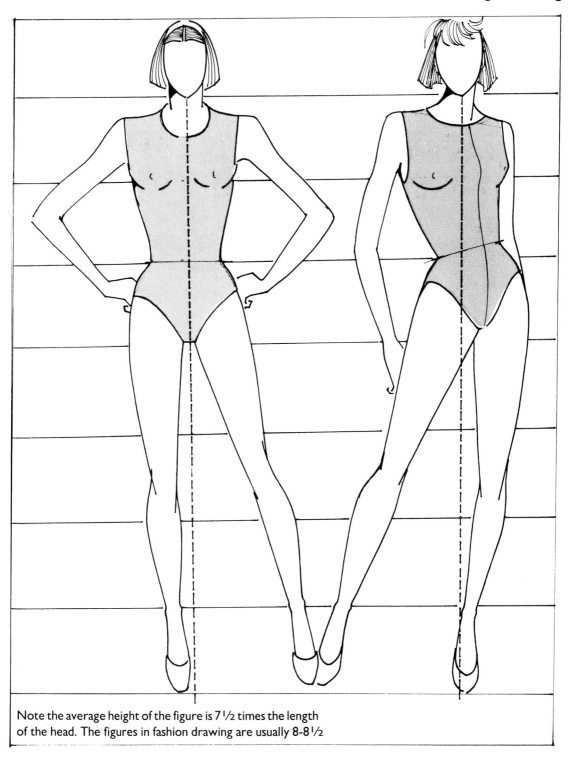

Note the average height of the figure is 7 1/2 times the length
of the head. The figures in fashion drawing are usually 8-8 1/2

Figure drawing

Note the centre front line of the figure is indicated
as a guide when balancing the design details

Sketches illustrating the one pose used to sketch
three different design shapes

Figure drawing

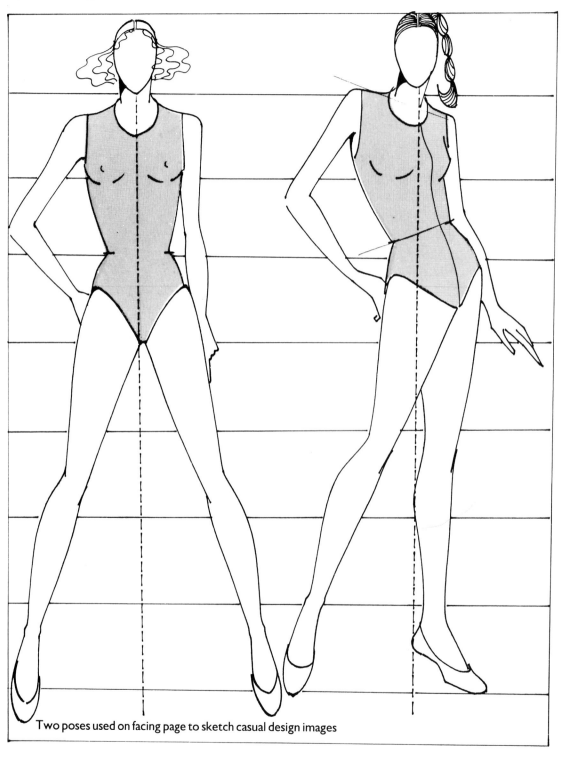

Two poses used on facing page to sketch casual design images

Figure drawing

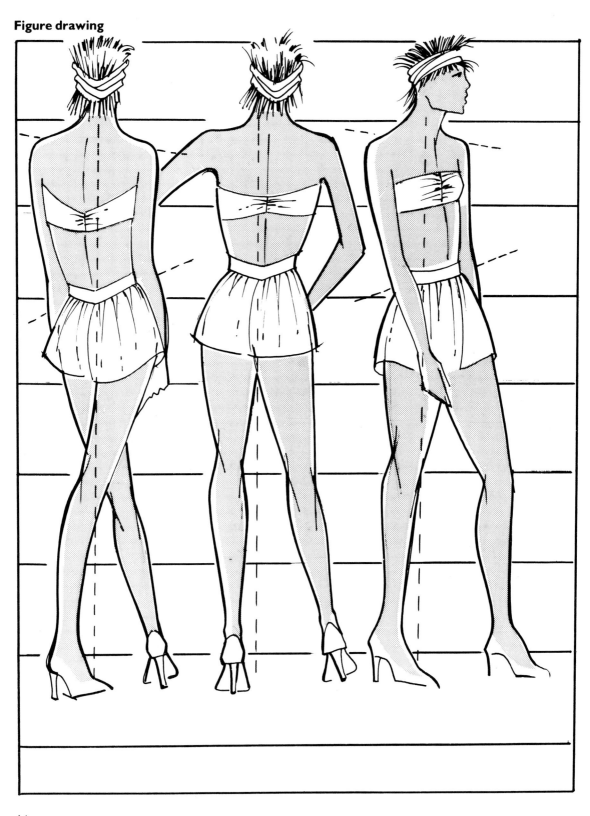

Three design sketches using the templates

Figure drawing

Fashion templates for men's wear designs

Figure drawing

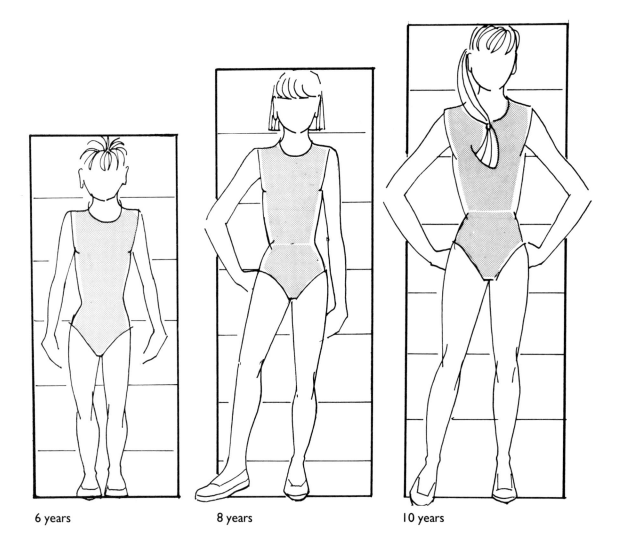

6 years   8 years   10 years

When drawing children and designing for different age groups it is important to be aware of the changing proportions of the growing child.

The method illustrated will help the student to sketch the figure and work out the correct proportions related to the age.

20

12 years   15 years   18 years

Appliqué

This effect is produced by applying pieces of fabric of different shapes and sizes to the surface of another fabric. The fabric pieces may vary in colour, pattern and texture. The technique varies from machine to handwork.

The design and use of appliqué should be carefully planned, bearing in mind the surface fabric on which the decoration is to be applied. Consideration should also be given to the colour, size, balance and proportion of the appliqué design related to the entire garment. The designs may be bold and simple as often used on leisure and beach wear, and on

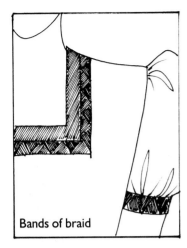

Bands of braid

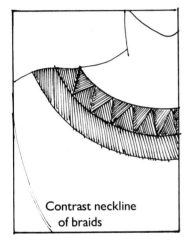

Contrast neckline of braids

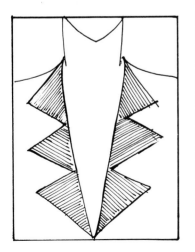

Appliqué leaf shapes and lace

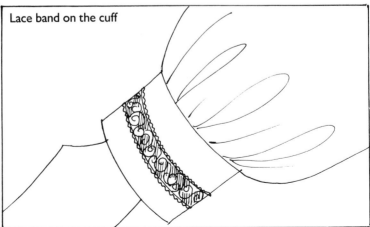

Lace band on the cuff

Appliqué

children's garments. More delicate designs are needed for use on lingerie, day and evening wear.

Many embroidery techniques may be combined with appliqué work eg quilting, beading and machine embroidery. The materials used may be fabric, felts, leathers, net or lace.

Printed fabric, applied net with machine embroidery

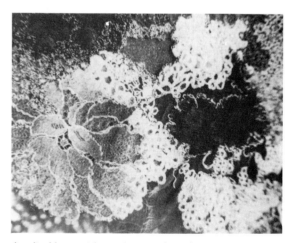

Applied lace with machine embroidery

Fashion sketches
Stylized sketches
Lace produced with a fine pen indicating the lace pattern. Faces and arms painted with water-colour wash. Faces only suggested

Appliqué designs with bold geometric shapes in contrasting fabrics and patterns, applied to children's play outfits

Belts

The belt as a fashion accessory has become a very important feature. It may be used as a detail, as part of a fashion image or as the main focal point of a design. The designs vary, depending on the image, from a casual sporty look to the sophisticated and classic designs. The shapes change from large bold designs with a variety of fastenings to the more delicate and understated effects.

The fastenings may be buckles, clasps, ties, lacing, hooks, studs or slotted straps and many ingenious ideas have been designed to achieve a desired effect. The materials may be selected from a large range of leathers of different colours and textures to the use of fabric, rubber, metal or a combination of different materials.

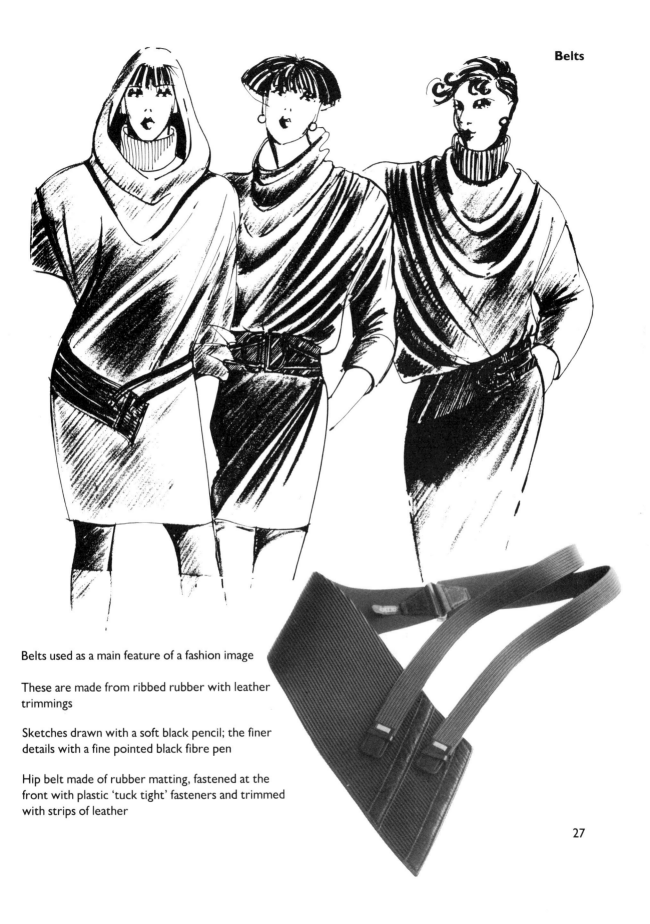

Belts used as a main feature of a fashion image

These are made from ribbed rubber with leather trimmings

Sketches drawn with a soft black pencil; the finer details with a fine pointed black fibre pen

Hip belt made of rubber matting, fastened at the front with plastic 'tuck tight' fasteners and trimmed with strips of leather

27

Belts

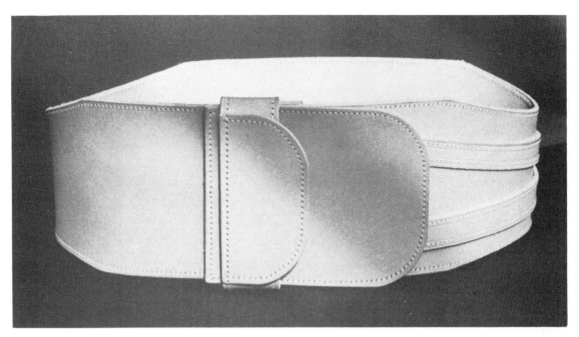

Wide leather belt with strap side fastening, featuring
top stitching

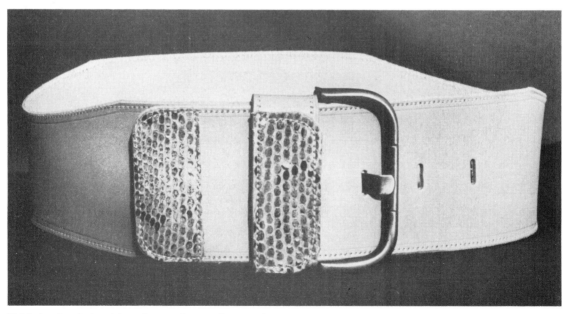

Wide leather belt with python on keeper loop and
belt end

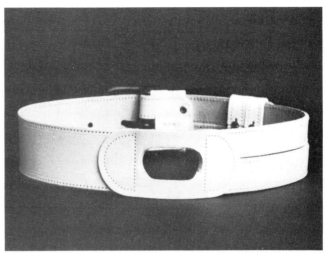

Leather belt divided at the back into a double strap on one side and fastened at the front with a simple buckle

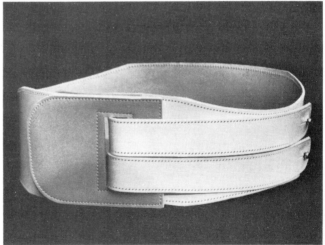

Wide shaped belt with double straps fastened with collar studs

Fashion sketch
Sketch produced with a black wax crayon. The texture of the dress has been achieved by placing the paper over a textured surface

29

Belts

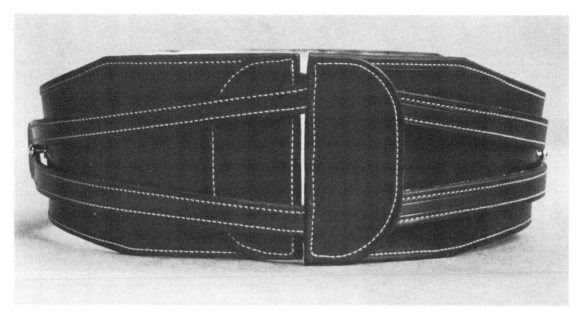

Fifties style wide cinched waisted leather belt with
contrast white saddle stitching. Cross-over double
straps are featured at the side fastened with collar
studs

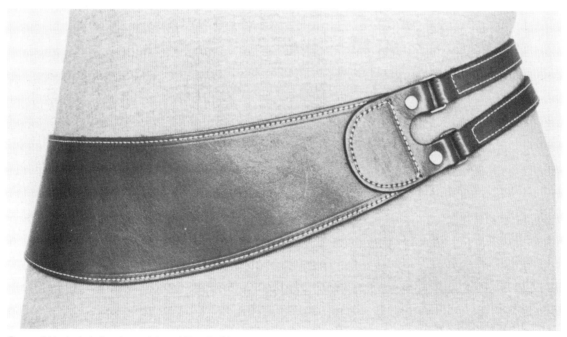

Curved hip belt in leather with saddle stitching as a
feature

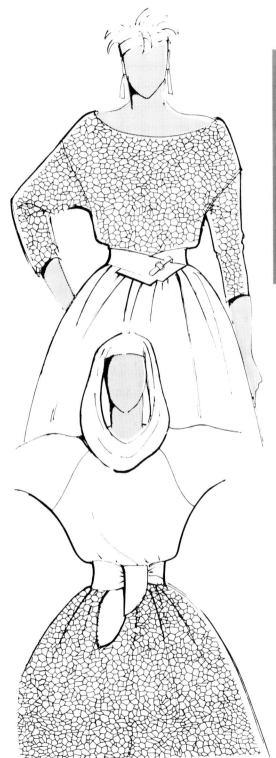

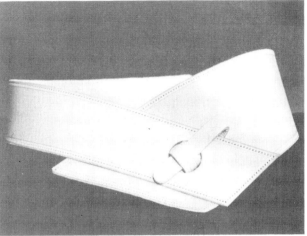

Asymmetrical cross over hip belt fastened at the front with interesting loop feature

Fashion sketches
Simple stylized sketches produced with a black fine pointed pencil. The faces have been left out to give emphasis to the design. *Letratint* has been added for pattern effects

Soft suede tie belt with contrast double stitching

Belts

Soft reversible tie belts joined at the back with various decorative leather shapes

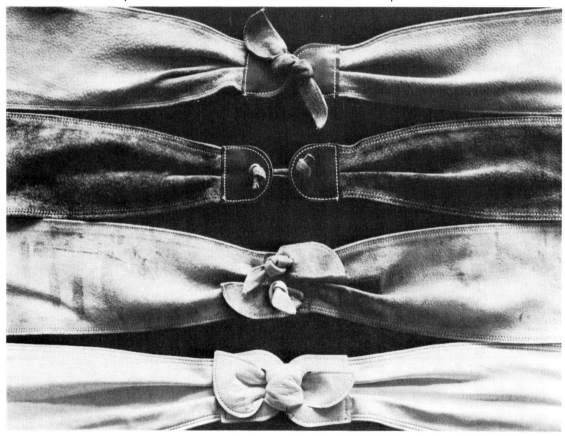

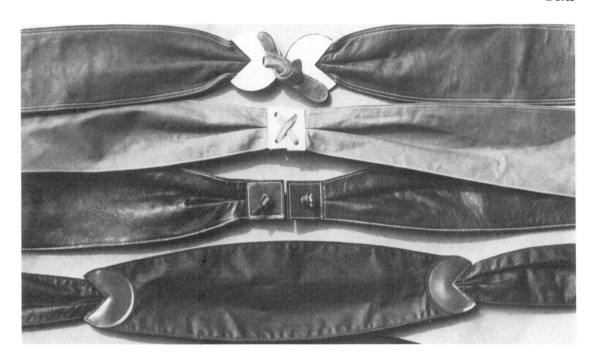

33

Bias cut

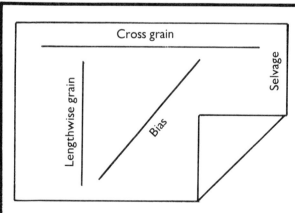

The grains of the weave indicate the direction of the yarn. Lengthwise is the *warp* and crosswise the *weft*. The diagonal which intersects these two grain lines is the *bias*. The crosswise grain has more 'give' and drapes well, achieving a fuller effect

A selection of designs illustrating the use of the bias cut

Draped neckline

Cowl neckline

Peplum

Extended shoulder

Godet in contrast fabric

Full skirt cut on bias

Bows

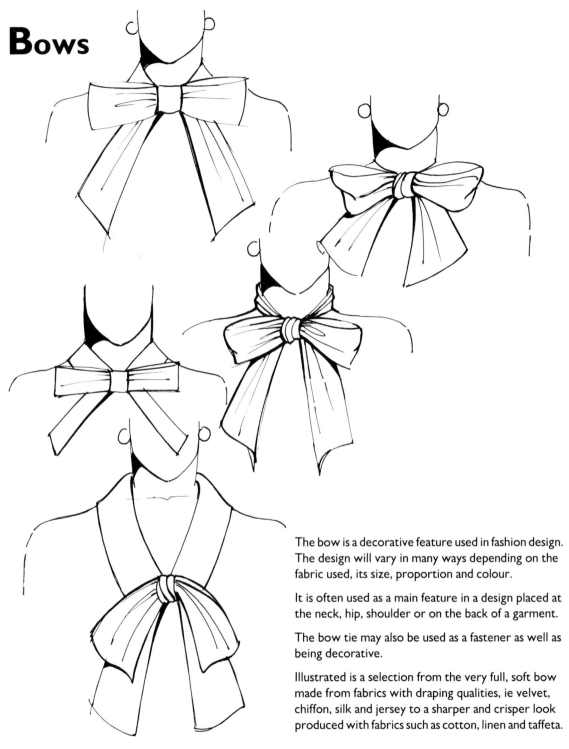

The bow is a decorative feature used in fashion design. The design will vary in many ways depending on the fabric used, its size, proportion and colour.

It is often used as a main feature in a design placed at the neck, hip, shoulder or on the back of a garment.

The bow tie may also be used as a fastener as well as being decorative.

Illustrated is a selection from the very full, soft bow made from fabrics with draping qualities, ie velvet, chiffon, silk and jersey to a sharper and crisper look produced with fabrics such as cotton, linen and taffeta.

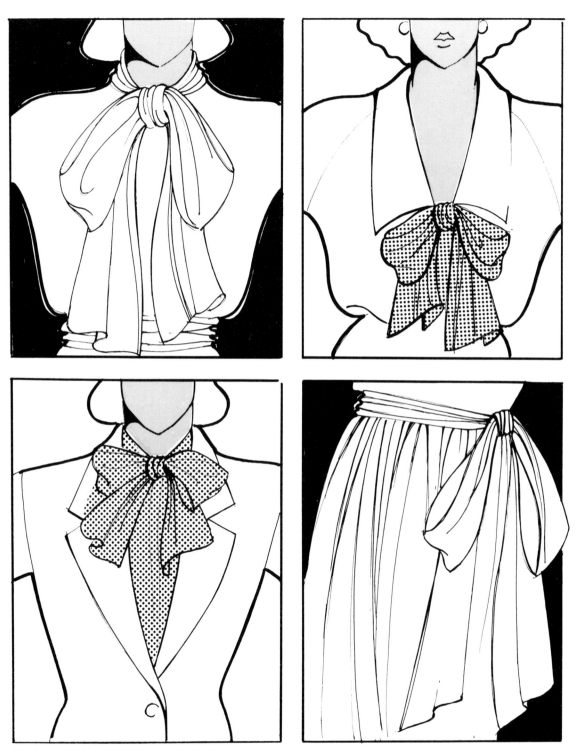

A selection of bows

Bows

Fashion sketches

Bows of different proportion made in a selection of
fabrics illustrating the way in which they drape

Bows

Sketching in two stages a large bow in a soft fabric

Large bows made in silk illustrating soft folds and drapes

A selection of bows incorporated in a design. Note
the variation of shape and drape of the bow

Collars

Sailor

Roll

Stand

Tailored

The designs of a collar are based on three basic styles. Flat, Stand or Roll. They may be attached to the neckline, detached or convertable. The weight and texture of the fabric used for the design will give different effects and this point should be carefully considered when producing design sketches.

In this section is illustrated a selection of designs adapted from the basic styles showing the use of the different styles on dresses, blouses and coats. Many variations may be developed from them.

Some of the designs have been taken from past periods of fashion with influences of military uniforms and national costumes. They are described for example as Peter Pan, Shawl, Mandarin, Sailor, Poets or Quaker depending on the origin of the collar. The design may be a practical feature used for protection, or purely decorative.

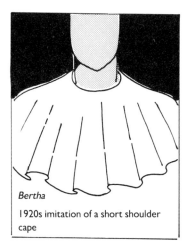

Bertha

1920s imitation of a short shoulder cape

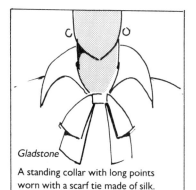

Gladstone

A standing collar with long points worn with a scarf tie made of silk. Made famous in the late nineteenth century by the Prime Minister, William Ewart Gladstone

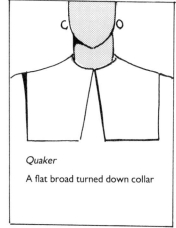

Quaker

A flat broad turned down collar

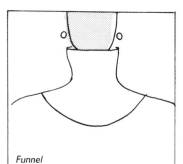

Funnel

This collar flares outward at the top of the neckline opening at the side or back

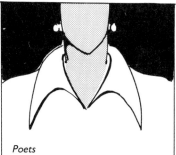

Poets

A collar made from a soft fabric attached to a shirt blouse, as often worn by poets such as Keats, Shelley and Byron

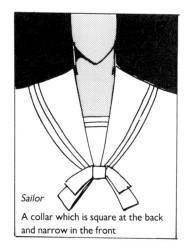

Sailor

A collar which is square at the back and narrow in the front

Eton

A large collar made from a stiffened white fabric as worn by students of Eton College

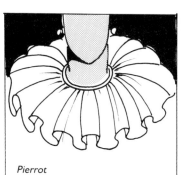

Pierrot

A very wide ruff of white fabric as worn by the French pantomime character, Pierrot

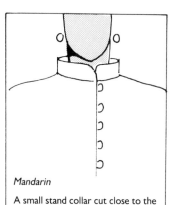

Mandarin

A small stand collar cut close to the neck

Collars

Terms used in describing parts of a collar
The *stand* is the part that fits close to the back of the neck. This part is covered by the turnover or fall. The height of the stand will vary depending on the design.

Fall is the part which falls over the stand

The *breakline* is the line on which the lapels turn back and the fall turns over the stand

The *style line* is the shape of the outer edge of the collar.

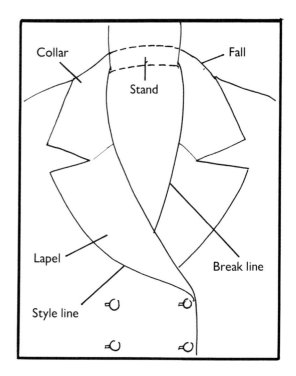

Two stages of drawing a double breasted collar and lapel on a coat. Note the dotted line showing the balance of the collar working from the centre front line

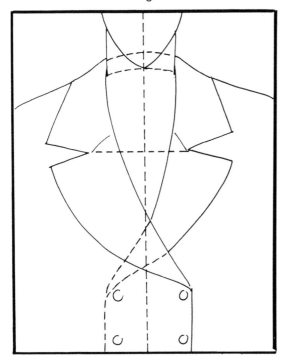

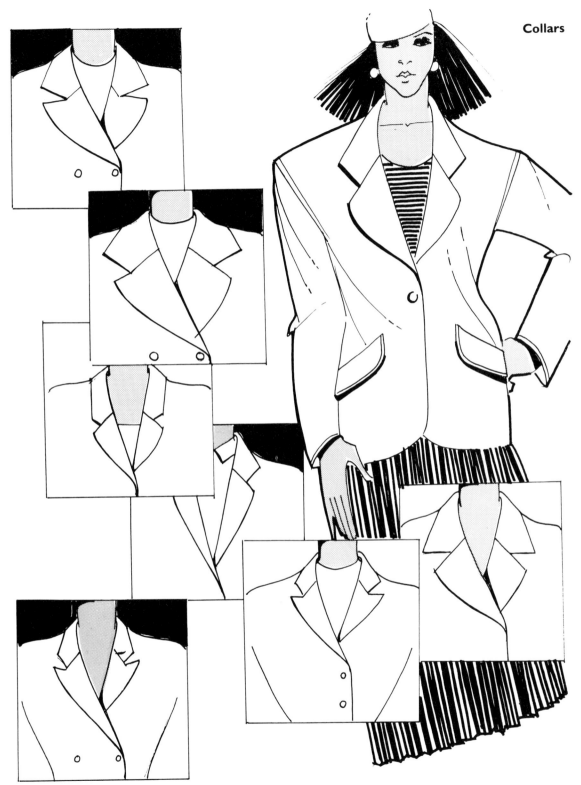

A selection of tailored collars and lapels

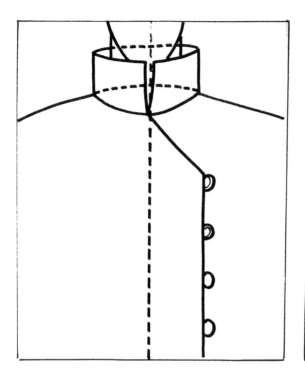

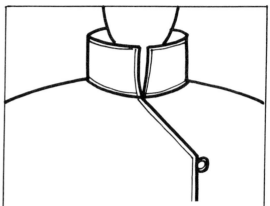

The stand. This collar extends above the neck seamline of the garment. The height will vary depending on the design effects required. It may be made from a single width band or a double width band which turns down on itself

This collar may be used on coats, suits, dresses or blouses. Note the two stages of drawing the standing collar

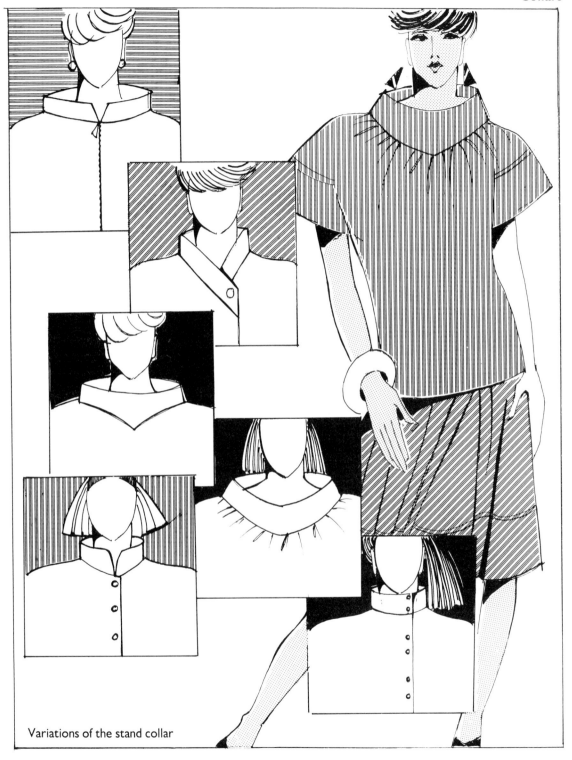

Variations of the stand collar

Collars

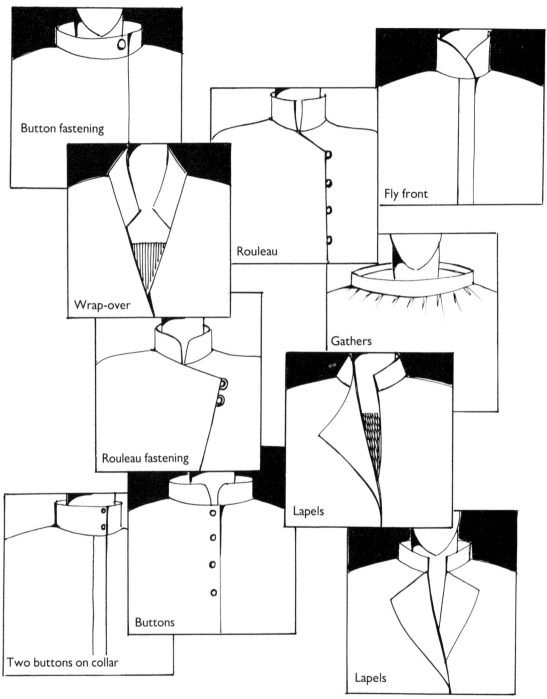

Button fastening

Fly front

Wrap-over

Rouleau

Gathers

Rouleau fastening

Lapels

Two buttons on collar

Buttons

Lapels

Stand collars combined with lapels, gathers and fastenings

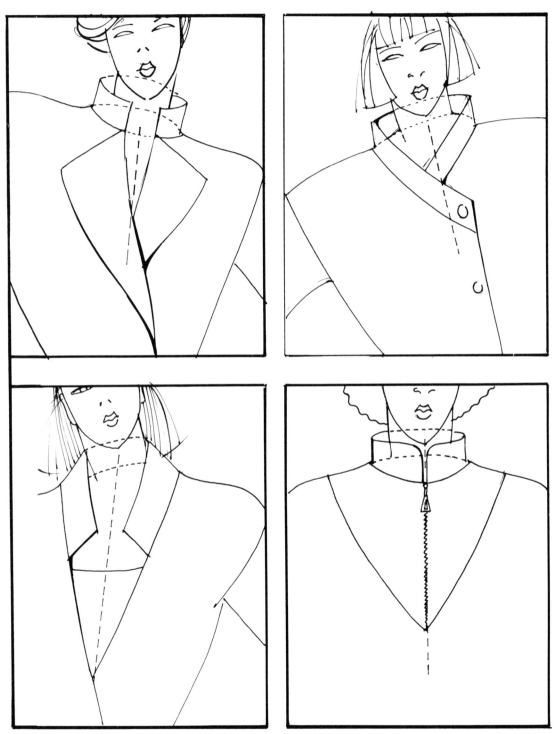

Designs showing the variations of a stand collar on a
selection of garments

Collars

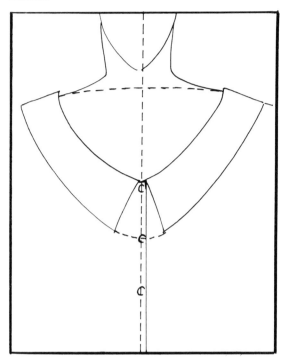
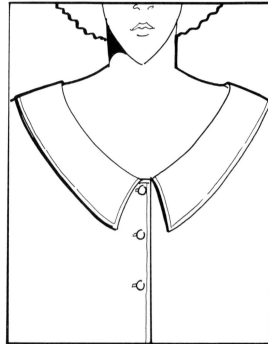

Two examples of the flat collar. Note the balance of
the button position from the centre front line

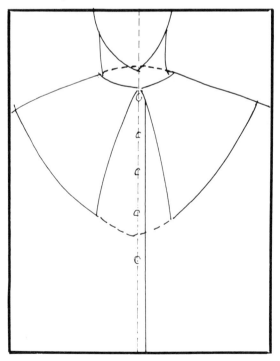

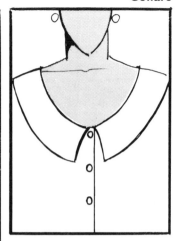

A flat collar is attached to the neckline to lay flat against the garment rising slightly about the neck edge. The Peter Pan collar is a good example of the flat collar. Variations from the basic flat collar are illustrated

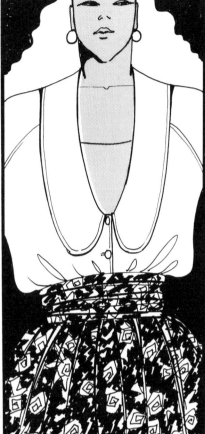

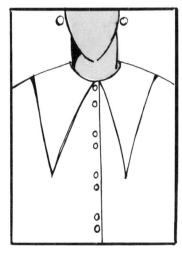

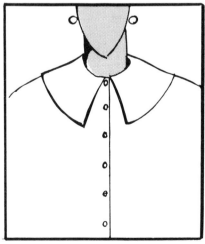

Collars

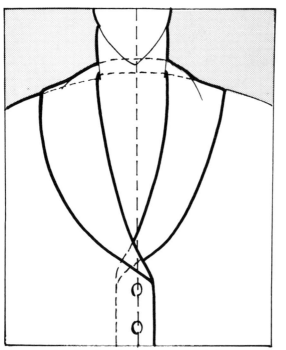

Drawing the shawl collar in two stages, balancing
from the centre front line

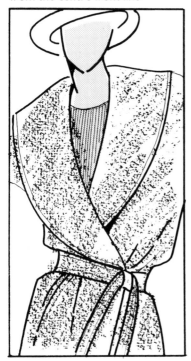
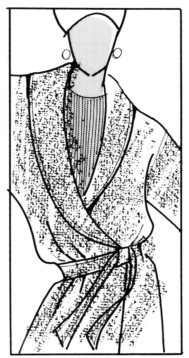
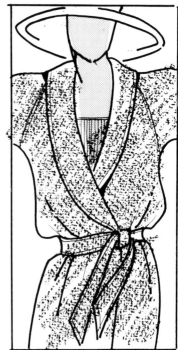

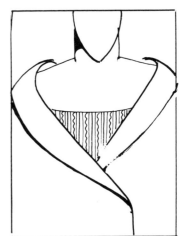

The shawl collar is cut in one single piece. This eliminates the need for the seam between the collar and the lapel. It is usually an unbroken line but in some designs it may be notched or scalloped. The design is usually a front wrapped garment held together by a belt in place of buttons, it may also be designed with other fastenings as illustrated on the facing page

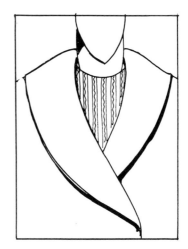

A selection of designs based on the shawl collar

Collars

Styles based on a funnel collar with zip fastener
openings

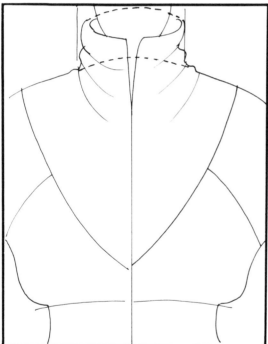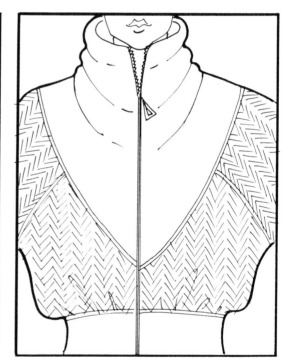

Two stages of drawing a funnel neck collar with zip
fastener opening

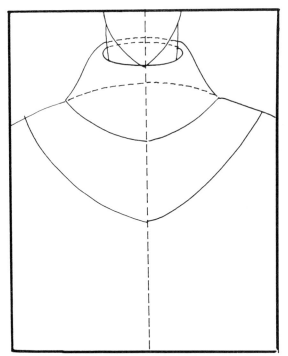

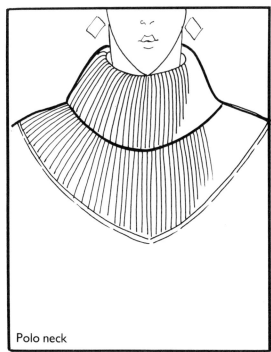

Two stages of drawing the polo neck

Polo neck

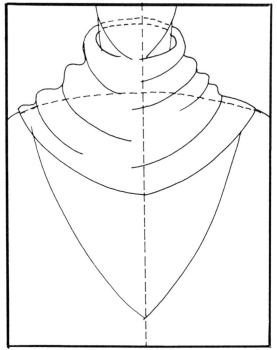

Two styles of drawing a turtle neck collar set into a
yoke with a centre front fastening

Turtle neck

Collars

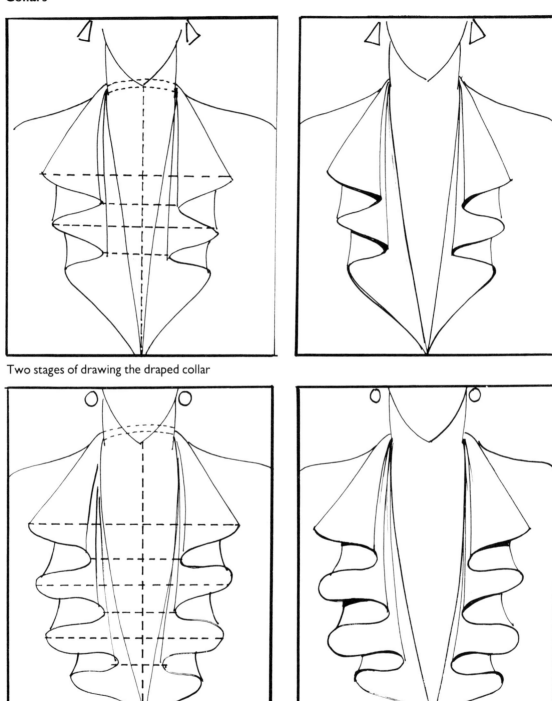

Two stages of drawing the draped collar

. . . note the dotted line used as a balance line when
sketching the folds of the flounce

Draped collars

Collars

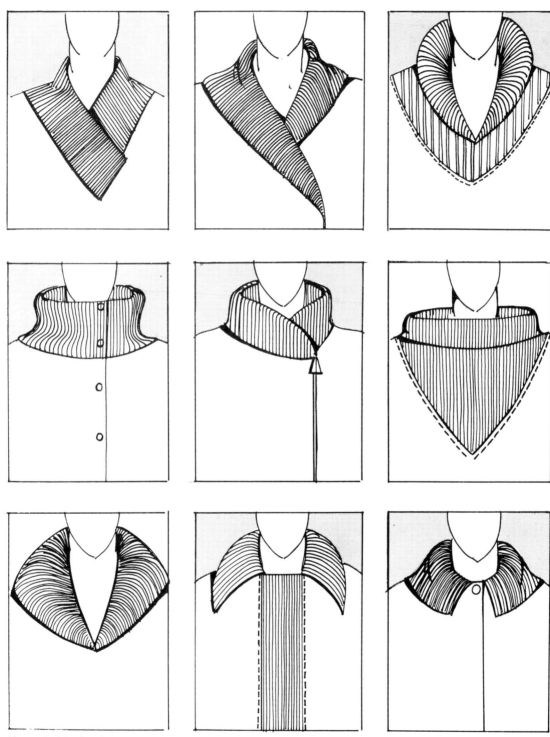

Knitted ribbed collars

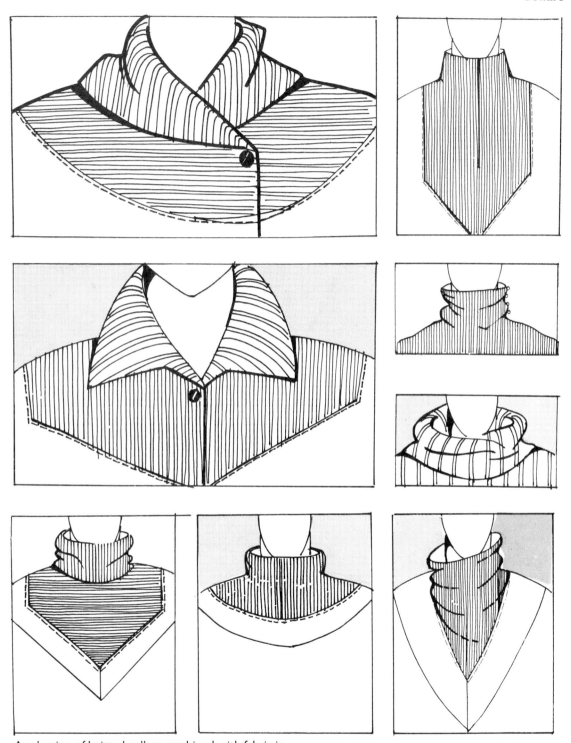

A selection of knitted collars combined with fabric in
a design. The effects vary depending on the yarns used

Collars

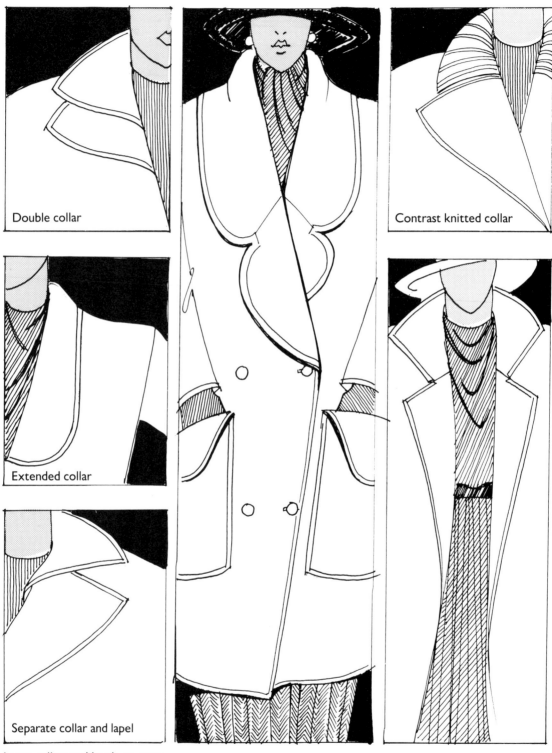

Double collar

Extended collar

Separate collar and lapel

Contrast knitted collar

Large collars and lapels on coats

60

Collars and lapels of different proportions suitable for
coats as a main feature of a design

Collars

A selection of collars and lapels

Collars and lapels

Collars

Collars and lapels

Collars and lapels

Collars

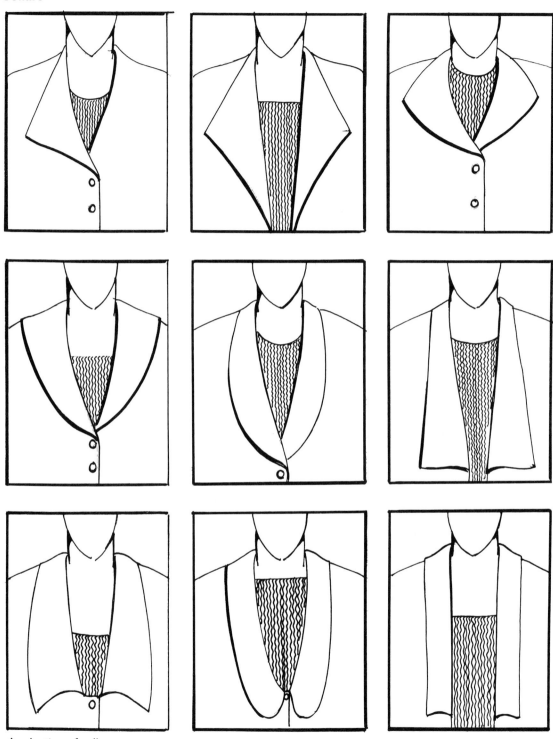

A selection of collars

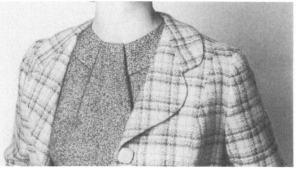

A selection of collars

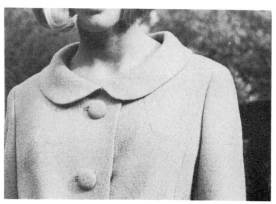

Cuffs

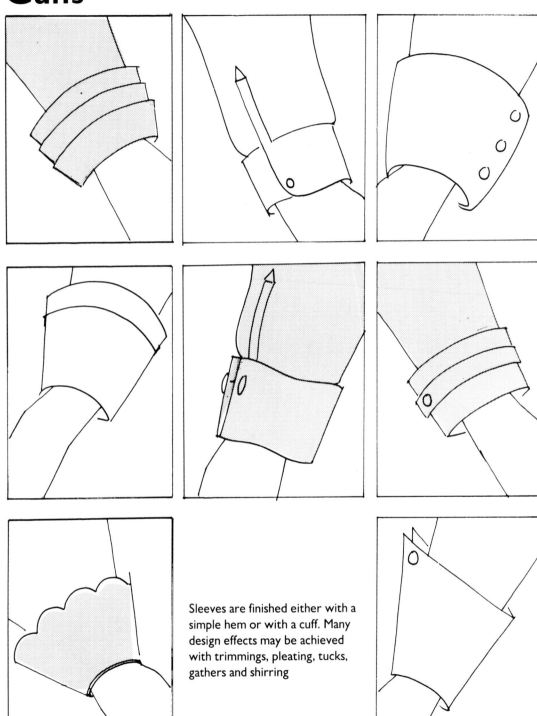

Sleeves are finished either with a simple hem or with a cuff. Many design effects may be achieved with trimmings, pleating, tucks, gathers and shirring

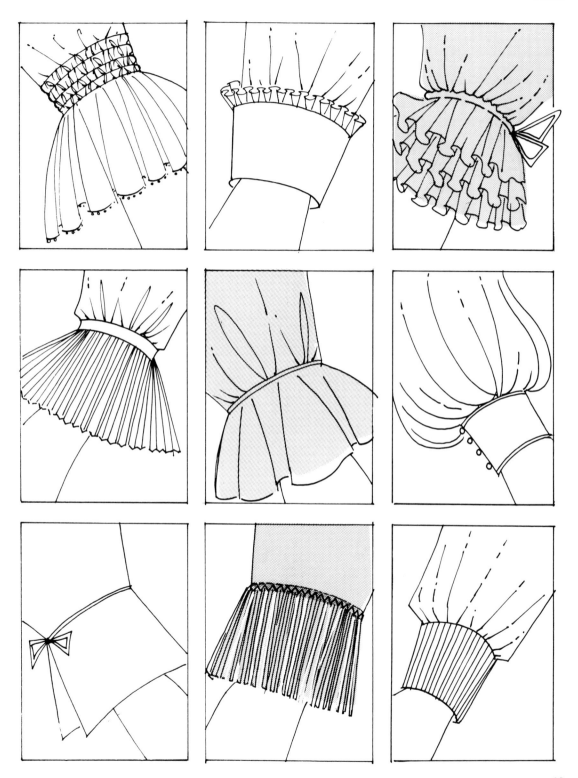

Drapes

Many effects may be achieved with the use of drapes within a design. They may be introduced as a complete theme or as a detail on the collar, bodice, sleeve or skirt.

The fabric used must have good draping qualities, ie silk, jersey, fine wool, velvet or chiffon. The drapes will vary from fine soft folds to very deep folds depending on the fabric.

Drapes

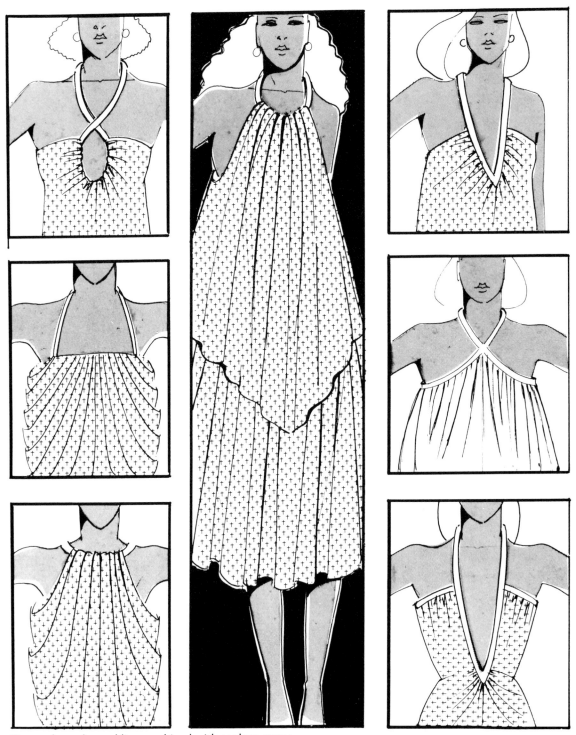

Drapes from the neckline combined with rouleau straps

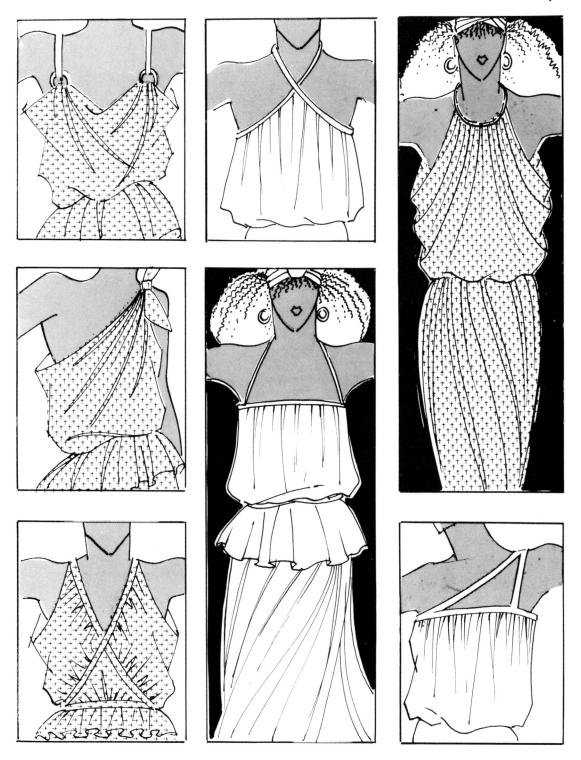

Drapes

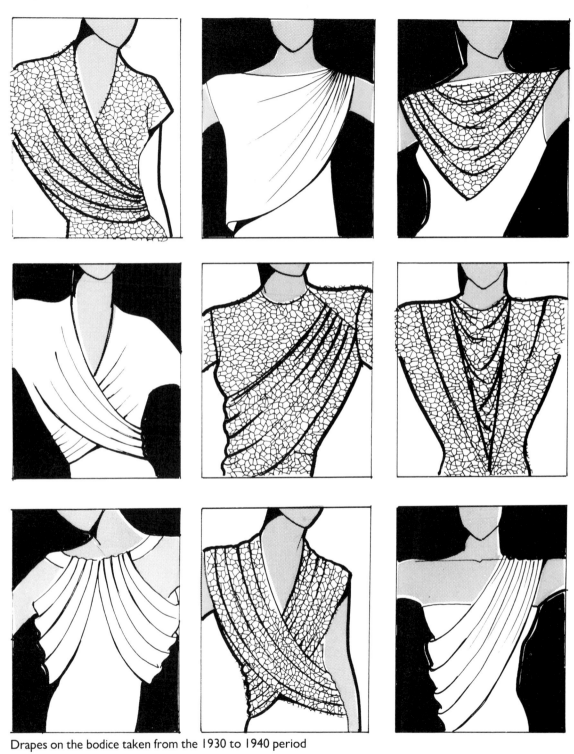

Drapes on the bodice taken from the 1930 to 1940 period

74

Two stages of sketching a draped evening dress

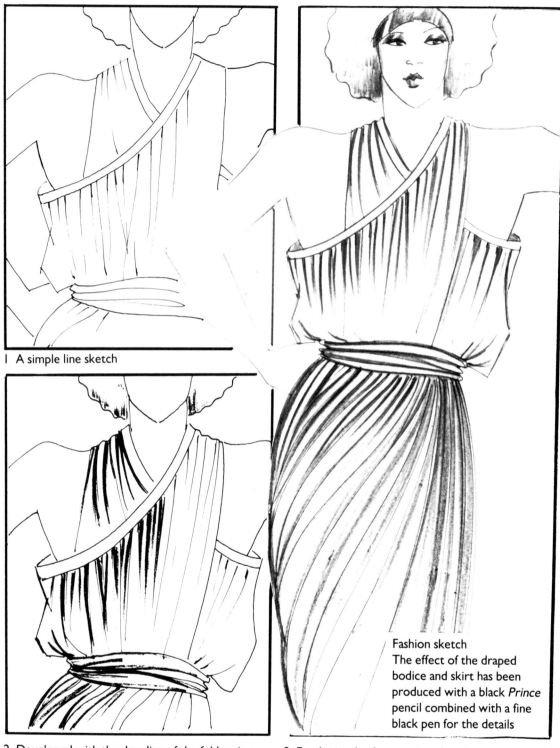

1 A simple line sketch

2 Developed with the shanding of the folds using a
soft pencil

Fashion sketch
The effect of the draped
bodice and skirt has been
produced with a black *Prince*
pencil combined with a fine
black pen for the details

3 Emphasise the drapes using a heavier pressure with
the pencil

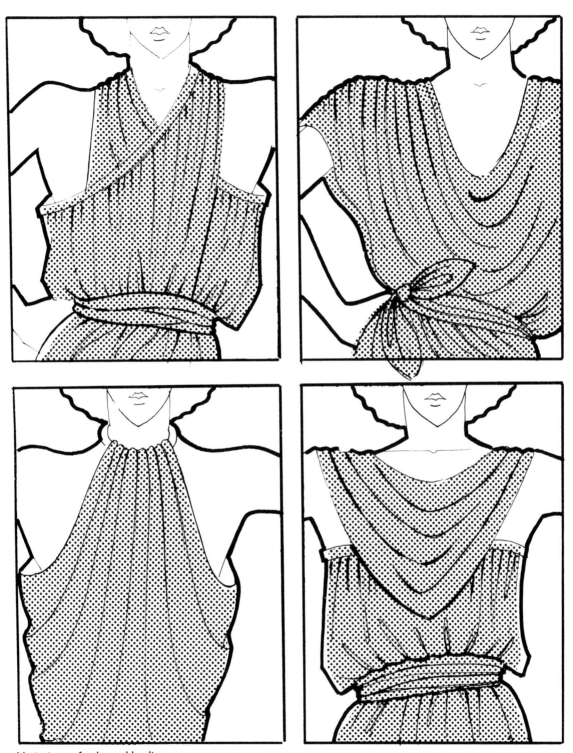

Variations of a draped bodice

Drapes

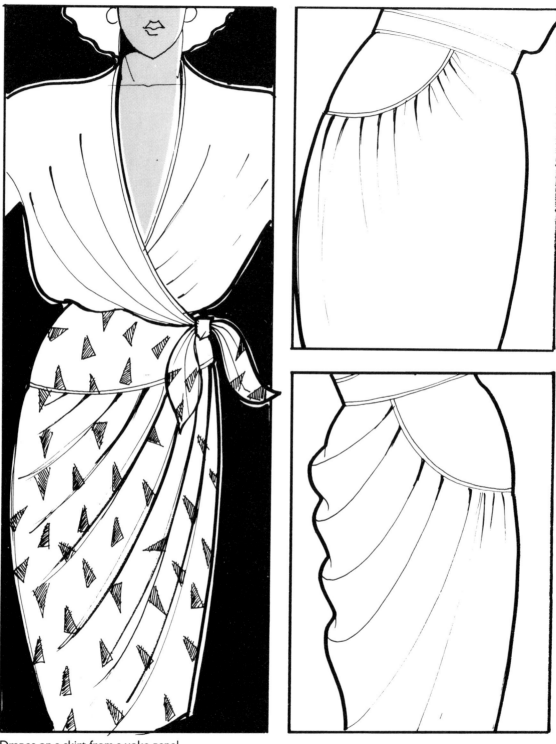

Drapes on a skirt from a yoke panel

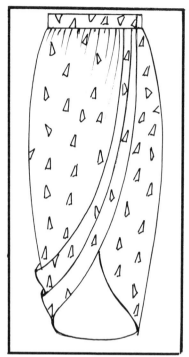
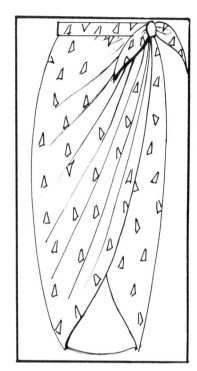

Wrap-over skirts incorporating drapes

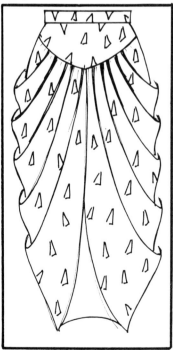

Variations of a draped skirt combined with a yoke panel

Drapes

A selection of dresses illustrating the use of the drape
introduced on the bodice, skirt or sleeve

A selection of dresses illustrating the use of the drape
introduced on the bodice, skirt or sleeve

Drawstrings

The drawstring is effectively used on many areas of a garment, ie hems of a jacket, blouses, necklines, sleeves and trousers.

A cord is inserted in the casing or hem to pull an area of fullness together. The cord may vary from piping, braid or rouleau.

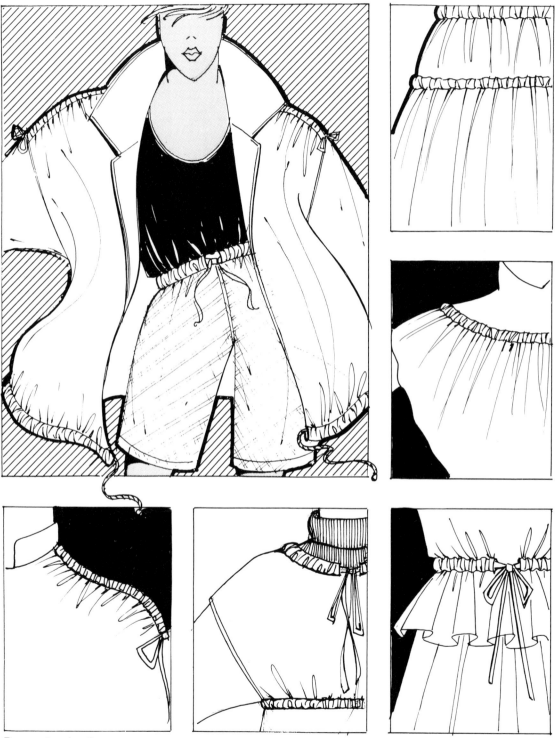

Drawstring details

Drawstrings

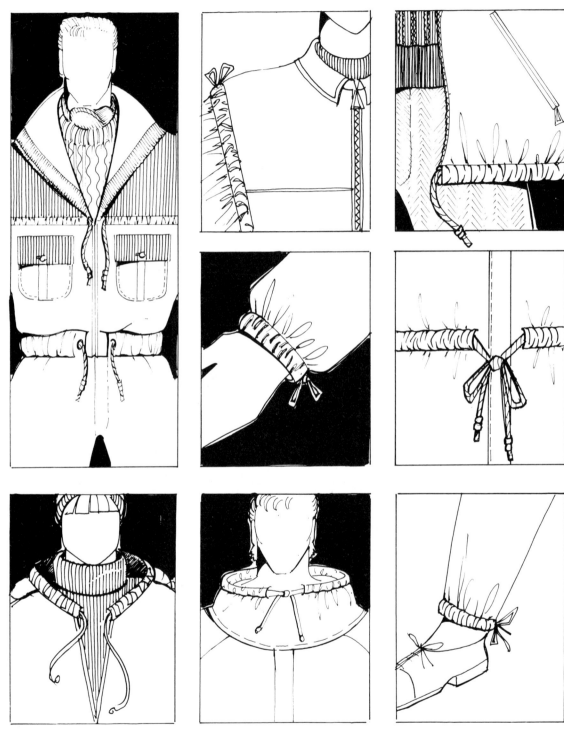

Drawstrings

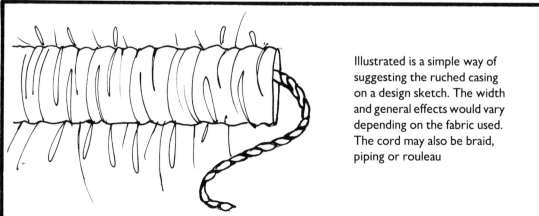

Illustrated is a simple way of suggesting the ruched casing on a design sketch. The width and general effects would vary depending on the fabric used. The cord may also be braid, piping or rouleau

Embroidery

The effects of embroidery are many, producing a variety of decorative effects on a design.

Different techniques are often used together to produce imaginative designs. Illustrated is a selection of samples showing the use of tambour beading, sequins, machine and hand embroidery. The samples shown are combined with fabric dye, printing, smocking, quilting and appliqué work.

By hand

Stitches breakdown into five basic stitch structures: knotted, flat, crossed, looped and composite.

There are many variations from which to select. Some are universal and others of a more local character.

By machine

Many effects are produced with the machine using attachments to produce different decorative effects.

Fashion sketches
The sketches
have been
produced with a
fine pointed pen for the details with white paint for
the highlights of the beading. The coat has been
coloured with a *Pantone* marker

90

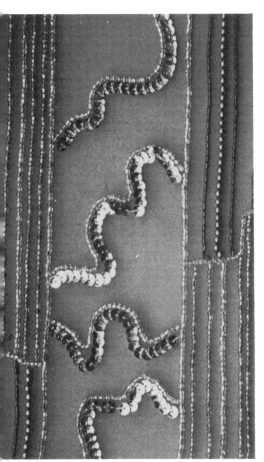

Sequins are stamped out of cellulose or plastic. They are made flat or cupped to reflect or catch the light and many be arranged in different ways depending on the effects required.

They may be scattered all over the fabric or applied to highlight certain areas of a design.

In some designs the entire fabric is built up with sequins overlapping each other, providing a rich effect.

Embroidery

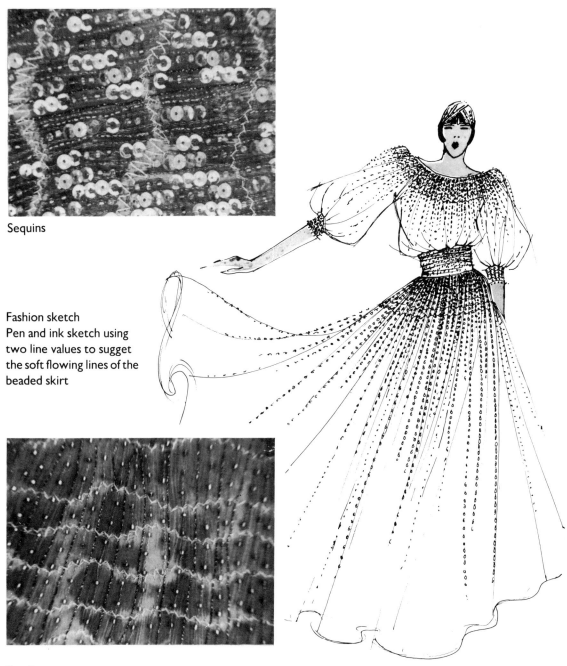

Sequins

Fashion sketch
Pen and ink sketch using
two line values to sugget
the soft flowing lines of the
beaded skirt

Beading

Beads can be used to great decorative effect in many ways. They are often used to enrich a fabric design or arranged on a plain fabric to add interest.

The selection of beads available is very wide. They are made in different shapes and sizes from a variety of materials including glass, plastic or wood.

Embroidery

Tambour beading
and thread work

Tambour beading

In this technique of beading the beads are applied with a tambour hook onto a tightly stretched fabric on a frame.

Fashion sketches
A fine *Rotring* pen has been used to suggest the tambour beading, combined with a black *Pantone* marker for the folds of the skirt

93

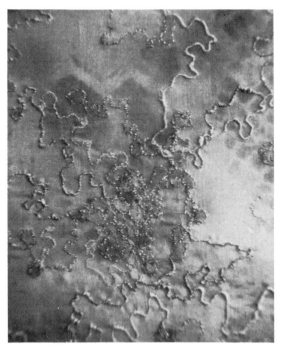

Small pieces of bonded silk organza on printed silk enriched with cable stitch

Sprayed fabric with a cutwork edge, embellished with Singer Irish satin stitch and tambour sequins

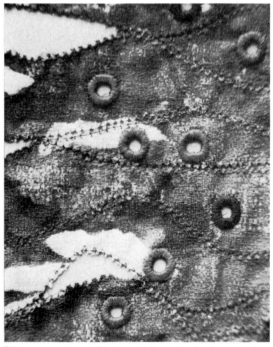

Silkscreen printed fabric with hemstitched cutwork and eyelets

Individually made Suffolk Puffs, hand printed and joined together, enriched with silk tassels

Tambour beading

Tamboured metallic thread work and hemstitching on silkscreen printed fabric

Fashion sketches
Flesh tinted with a *Pantone* marker. Outline of figures, beading and stitching with a fine pointed pen

Cornely chain and hemstitching

Machine embroidery dyed fabric

Embroidery

Stencil printing on black fabric enriched with Singer Irish machine embroidery using a variety of multicoloured threads

Machine embroidery

Sprayed and bonded
appliqué with machine
embroidery

Fashion sketches
Detail of embroidery produced with a fine *Rotring*
drawing pen and water-colour wash
When working on embroidery and beading it is only
required to suggest the effects. Make sure the
design is taken down to scale

Tambour beading
and thread work

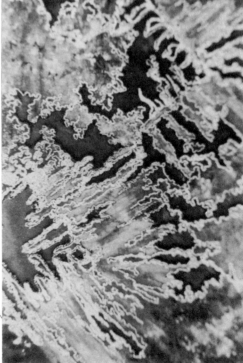

Machine
embroidery

Fasteners and fastenings

The range of fasteners from which to select is considerable from a large selection of buttons made from a variety of different materials to zips, press studs, *Velcro*, ties, hooks, clasps, clips, buckles and straps.

Their use may vary from being concealed and purely functional to being emphasised and used as a decorative main feature of a design.

A selection of fasteners has been illustrated to show how they may be used in relation to a design. The materials from which they are made may be metal, wood, plastic, leather or fabric.

Types of fasteners

Snap fasteners

These may be obtained in many sizes. They may be used as a decorative feature as well as being functional. They look very effective when introduced on sports wear and industrial garments. These are press studs usually made of metal and which may subsequently be covered with fabric.

Straps and buckles can be made in self material or contrasting with buckles of wood, metal, plastic, etc.

Lacing

Lacing is drawn through eyelets. The thickness of the lacing and eyelets vary. The way in which the lacing is tied will vary depending on the design effect required.

Zip fasteners (see also Zips)

Zip fasteners vary in width and length. They are made of metal or nylon. Many variations are produced in different weights of slides and colour.

Rouleau fastenings

These are rolls or folds of fabric, used for making loops and piping for fastening.

Frog fastenings

These may be made from cording or braid.

Loop button holes

Loops of cord or self fabric serve as a button hole.

Button snaps

Velcro

Velcro is made of two strips of fabric varying in width. One strip is covered with hooks and the other with very fine loops. When the two strips are pressed together the hooks engage the loops and give a very secure fastening which can be easily opened by a pulling action. This fastening is often used on sports and industrial garments as it is both functional and adaptable when used at the neck, cuffs pockets.

Button loops

Button loops may be substituted for button holes, the button loop may be set into the seam at the edge of the garment where the opening is placed or a frog fastener may be used which is more decorative.

Button loops are made of fabric tubing, self filled or corded. The thickness of the loops varies according to the button used, the fabric and placing.

Any buttons may be used with the loop fastener. The most popular are ball buttons, usually covered in the same fabric as the garment. Chinese ball buttons are made with a length of round cord.

Drawstring and casing (see Drawstring)

A drawstring and casing. The casing is used to accommodate a drawstring or elastic. It can be used in may ways and looks effective on a design as illustrated. This fastener is decorative as well as being functional.

Braces and buckels

Bows (see Bows)

The bow consists of knotted ends of fabric. It drapes better when cut on the bias with the ends cut at an angle. It is often used at the neck of a dress or blouse or at the waist as a belt, which may be purely decorative or serve as a fastener.

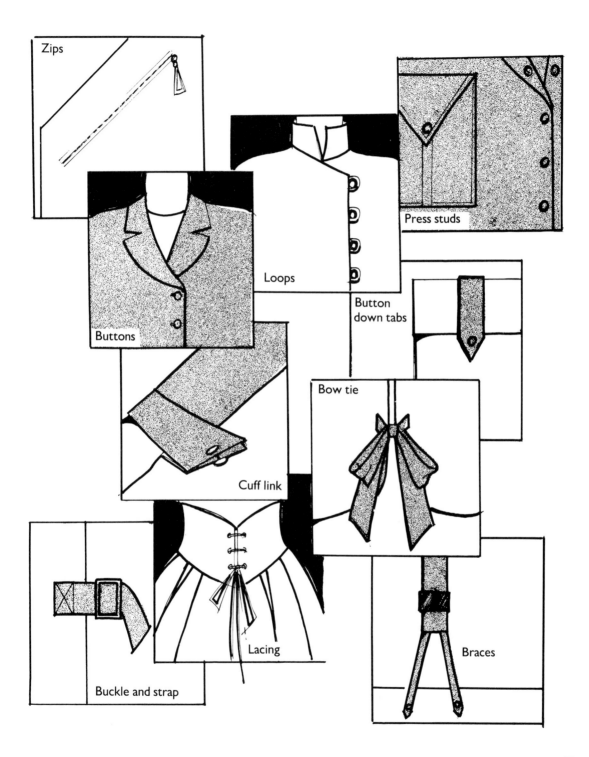

Zips

Press studs

Loops

Button down tabs

Buttons

Bow tie

Cuff link

Buckle and strap

Lacing

Braces

Fastenings

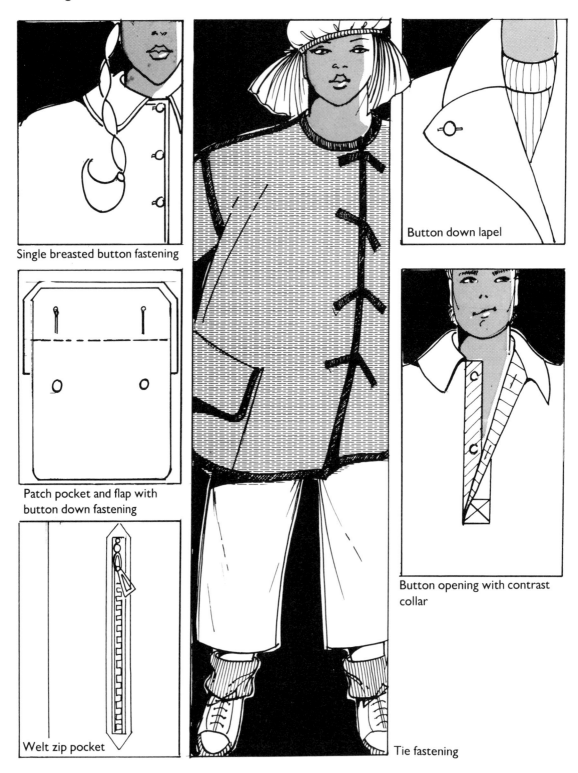

Single breasted button fastening

Patch pocket and flap with
button down fastening

Welt zip pocket

Button down lapel

Button opening with contrast
collar

Tie fastening

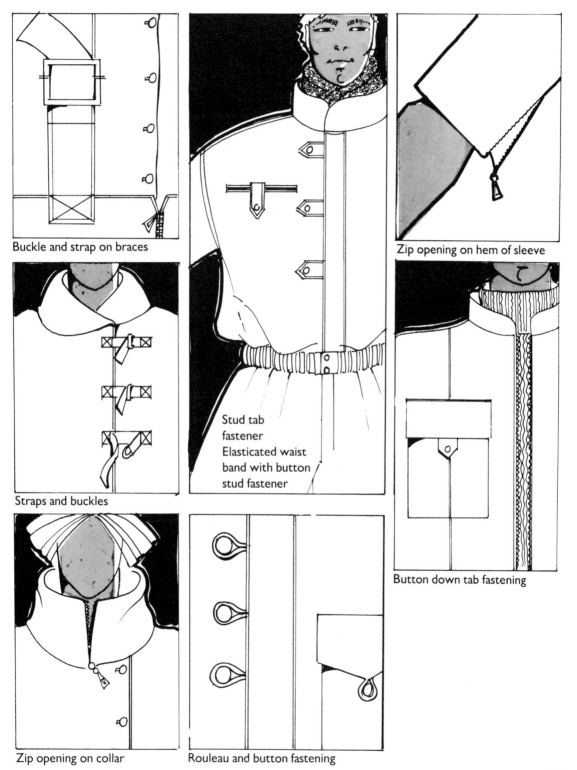

Buckle and strap on braces

Zip opening on hem of sleeve

Straps and buckles

Stud tab
fastener
Elasticated waist
band with button
stud fastener

Button down tab fastening

Zip opening on collar

Rouleau and button fastening

Fastenings

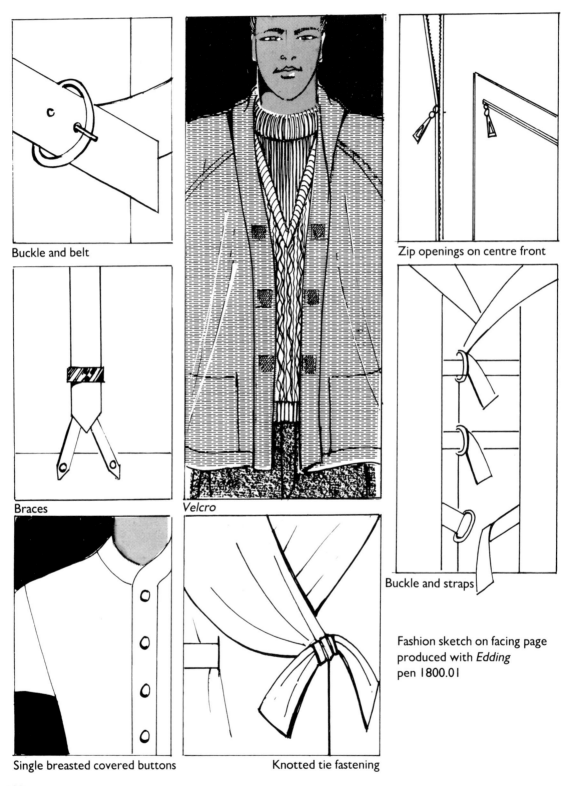

Buckle and belt

Braces

Velcro

Zip openings on centre front

Buckle and straps

Single breasted covered buttons

Knotted tie fastening

Fashion sketch on facing page
produced with *Edding*
pen 1800.01

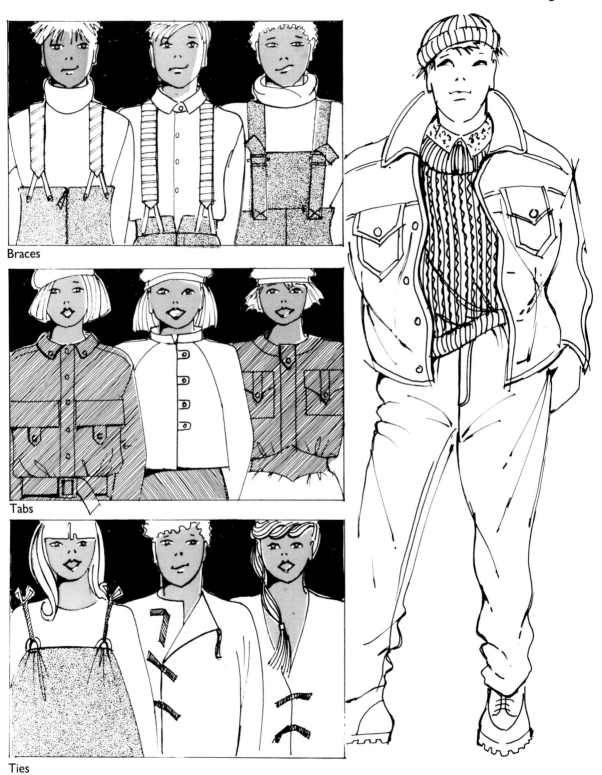

Braces

Tabs

Ties

Fastenings

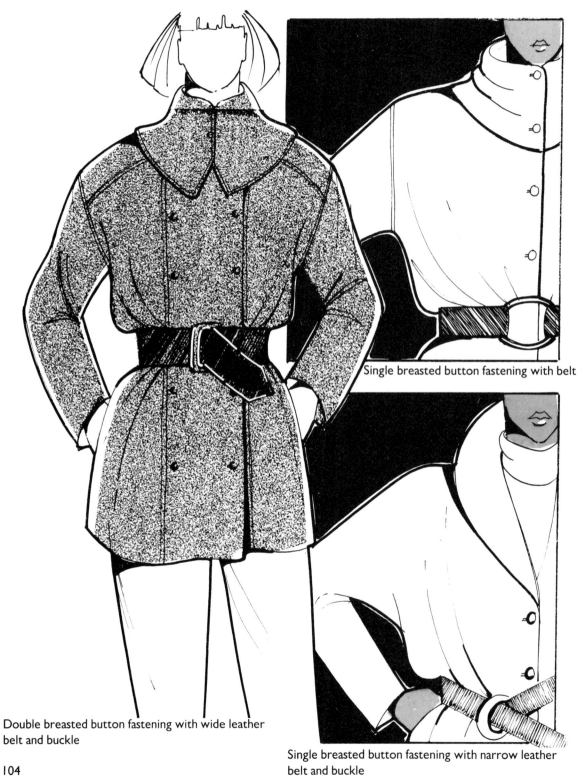

Single breasted button fastening with belt

Double breasted button fastening with wide leather belt and buckle

Single breasted button fastening with narrow leather belt and buckle

Belt in leather and soft suede

Belt in rubber with ribing

Soft draped belt in fine wool fabric

Fashion sketch
Produced with a wax crayon
and fine pen for details of
seams, collar and belt

Frills and flounces

Flounce at neckline
cut on the bias

Double
layered frills

The frill or flounce work at the neckline of a dress or on the hem of a sleeve or skirt adds an attractive feature to a design. Certain fabrics lend themselves to this decorative treatment. The effect may be a main feature of a design as on a full skirt, sleeves or neckline. The fineness of the fabric determines the amount of fullness the flounce or frill will take but it must be made in a soft fabric which falls naturally into folds. The flounce is cut from two circles. It is fully flared at the hem but keeps a smooth fitting line at the point at which it is attached to the garment.

Puff sleeves gathered into a band and frill

A selection of frills on necklines and sleeves

Frills and flounces

Illustration using a selection of black felt tipped pens
of different thicknesses

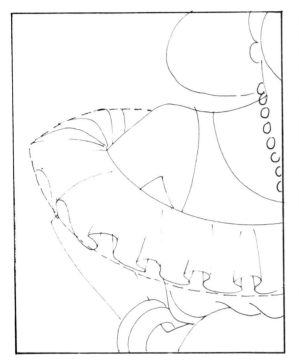

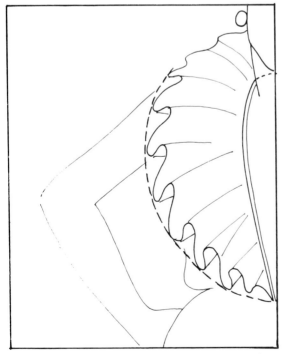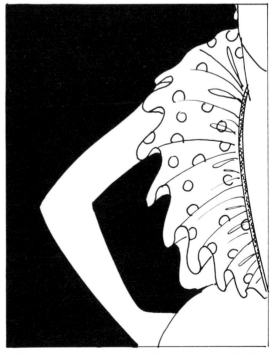

Illustrating in two stages the sketching of a large frill on the bodice. Note the dotted line indicating the balance of the hem. It is helpful to give yourself this guideline when sketching

Frills and flounces

A selection of frills in a soft fabric

Illustrating the construction lines for a design sketch.
Note how the frills always fall back on the hem line,
indicated with a dotted line

Frills and flounces

A selection of single and double frills on yokes, collars
and sleeves

A selection of collars made from frills and flounces
The sketch has been completed with the use of
Letratint – a fine transparent film – which is applied to
the sketch to add pattern and tone used for
illustrating for reproduction in print

113

Frills and flounces

Full flounced skirts

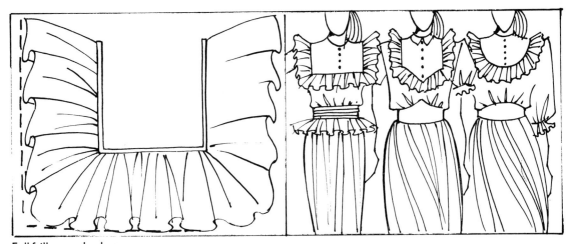

Full frills round yokes

Frills on hem of skirts

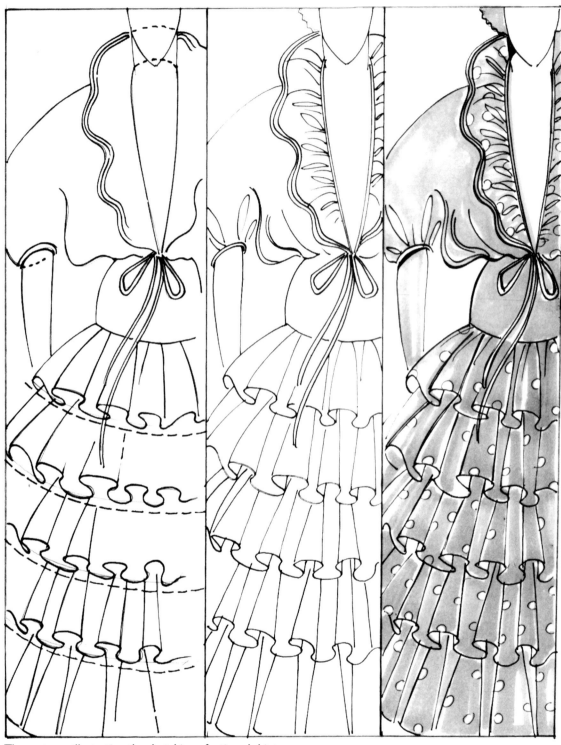

Three stages illustrating the sketching of a tiered skirt

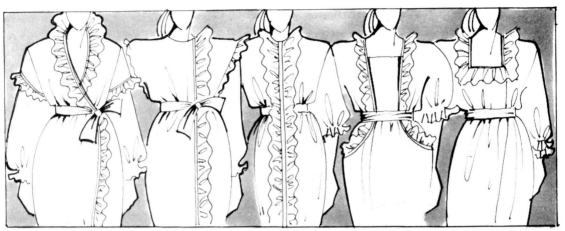

The use of frills on a design used at the neck, . . .

on the panel lines, edging of openings and sleeve hems

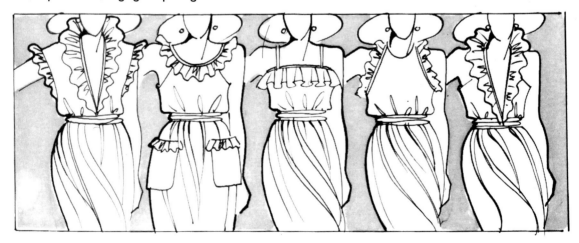

Frills and flounces

Edged organza frill set into a seam. The fabric of the garment has been sprayed, machine embroidered and tambour beaded

Picot edged, sprayed cotton organdie frills

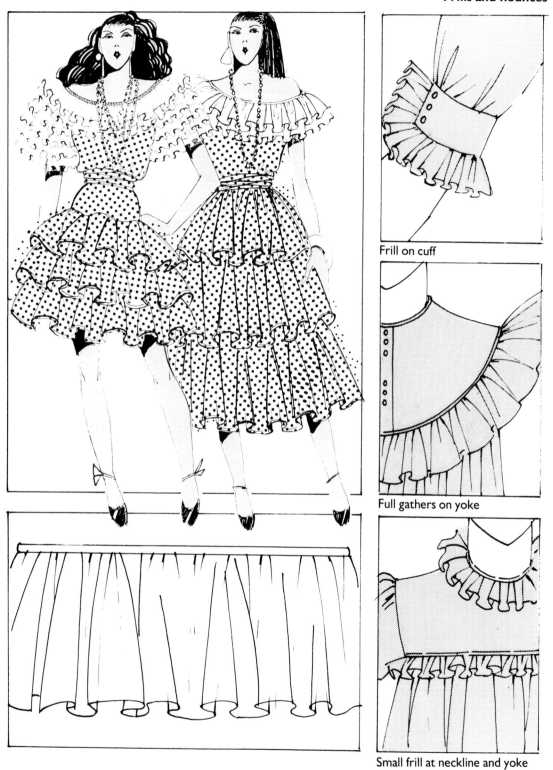

Frill on cuff

Full gathers on yoke

Small frill at neckline and yoke

119

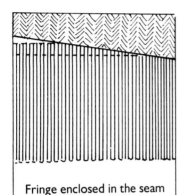

Fringe enclosed in the seam

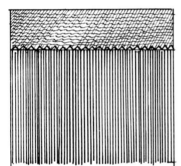

Fringe unravelled made from woven fabrics. To prevent any further unravelling a small zigzag stitch is used over the edge

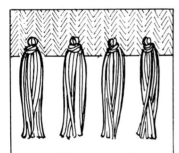

Knotted fringe used on a finished edge on woven fabrics making a hole for the knot between the threads

Fringing

Fringing is an attractive feature used in design. There are four types:
1 The fringe enclosed in the seam, 2 the self fringe from fabric unravelled, 3 the knotted fringe, 4 the very ornate fringe made from beads. Fringes need not be restricted to hems. They can also be applied to seams, collars, pockets, sleeves and skirts

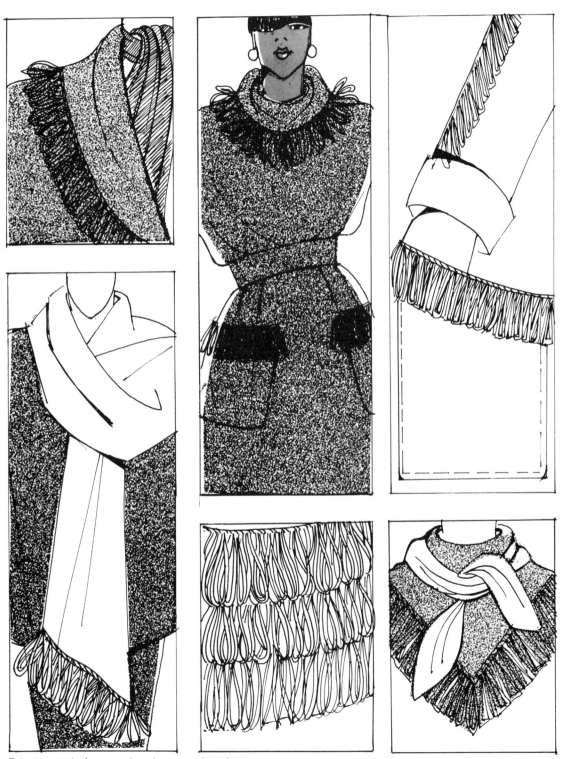

Fringing made from rouleau loops enclosed in a seam

Fringing

Leather fringe enclosed in seam

Fringe unravelled from the fabric hem

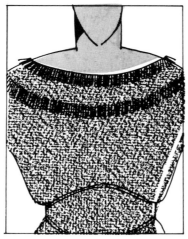

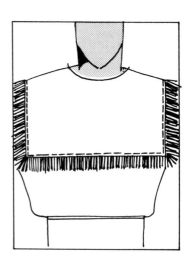

Fringing

A variation of fringe placement

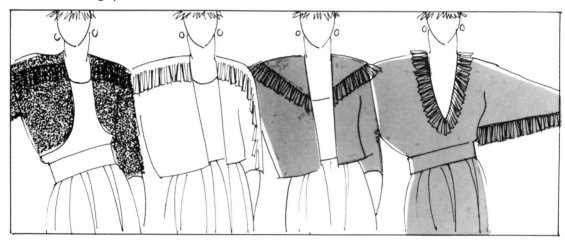

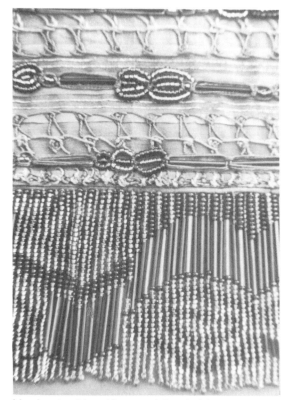

Hand embroidered hem with beaded fringe

Picot edged frills and beaded fringe

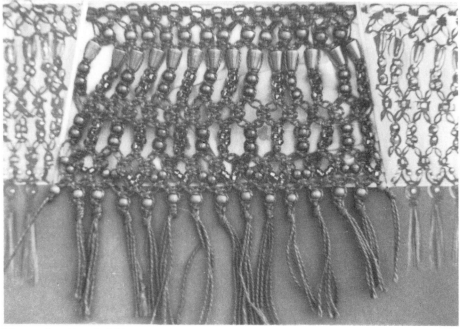

Macramé and beaded fringe

Fringing

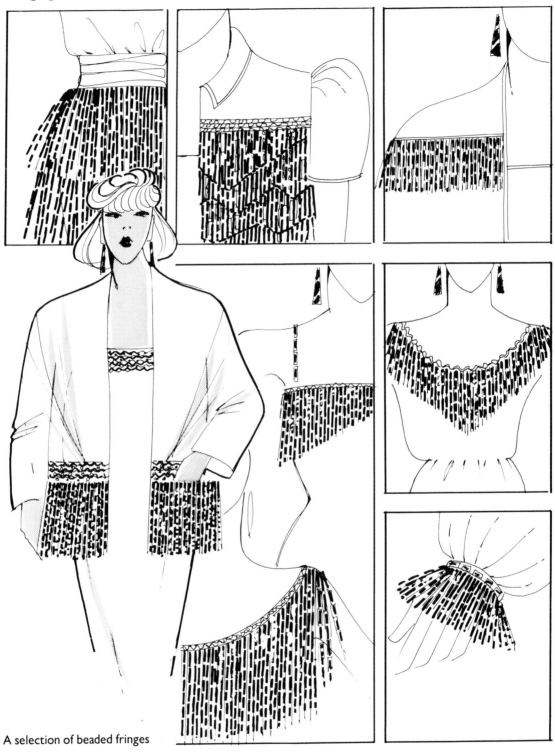

A selection of beaded fringes

Gathers

When designing, gathers are used in a variety of ways on different areas of a garment such as the yoke, sleeves, skirt or panel lines. They are often used as a detail on a pocket, cuff or peplum.

Gathering usually reduces to about one half or one third of the original width. Depending on the fabric being used for the design the effects will vary from very soft draped folds of jersey, silk or fine wool to the rich deep gathers produced with brocade, taffeta or cotton. The gathers fall best on the lengthwise grain of the fabric.

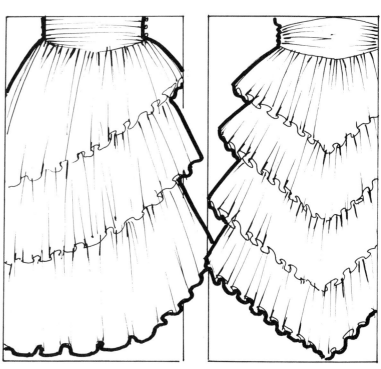

Gathers produced with a stiff cotton achieving a crisp and billowing effects on the hems of skirts, peplums and waistline

129

Gathers

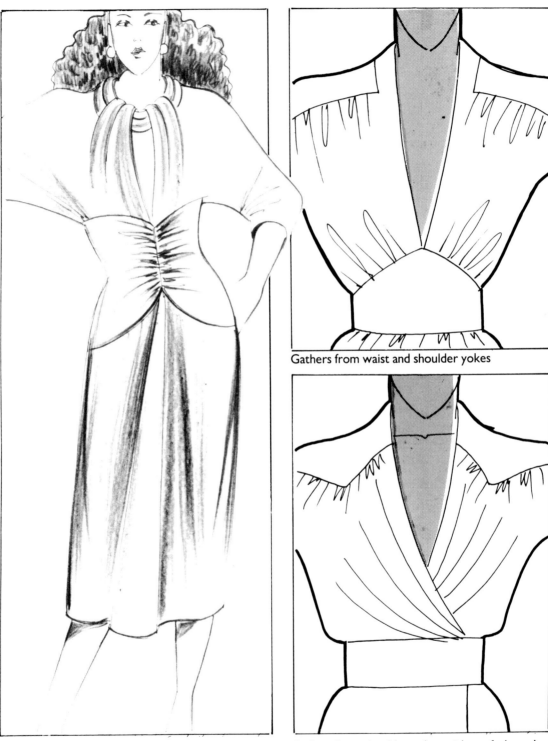

Gathers from waist and shoulder yokes

Fashion sketch produced with a felt tipped pen, and fine detail with a *Pentel Ultra Fine* pen

Gathers from shoulder yokes with a soft draped bodice.

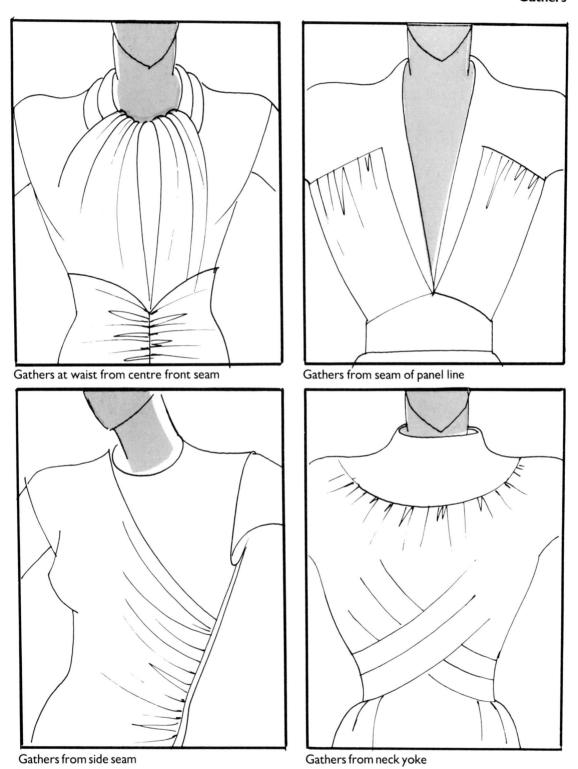

Gathers at waist from centre front seam

Gathers from seam of panel line

Gathers from side seam

Gathers from neck yoke

Gathers

Note the variation of the hem line of the fabrics
illustrated from a crisp cotton with deep folds to silk
and the soft folds of jersey

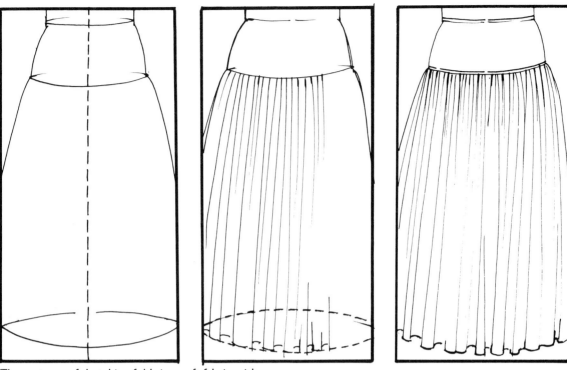

Three stages of sketching folds in a soft fabric with small delicate gathers

Three stages of sketching deeper folds of a stiffer and crisp fabric of cotton

Gathers

Folds in movement illustrating gathers from neck
lines, waist and skirt sections

Study the fall of fabric and the way in which it behaves when draped on a dress stand or model. This will help you considerably when sketching and developing ideas

Gathers

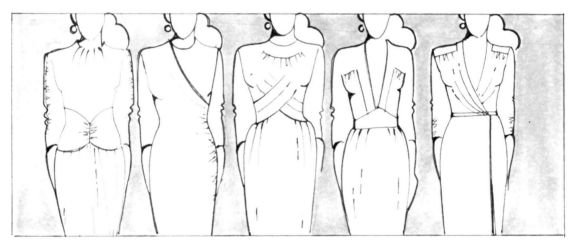

A variety of ways to introduce gathers into a design
of blouses, skirts and dresses

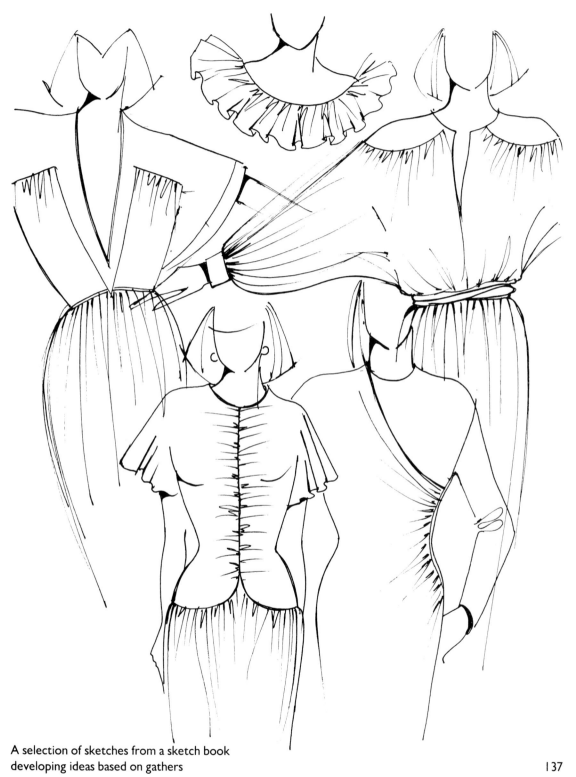

A selection of sketches from a sketch book
developing ideas based on gathers

Gathers

It's helpful to keep a sketchbook to refer to with sketches and notes of fashion details which may later by developed further

Fashion sketch

Produced with a *Finepoint* black
pen and a grey *Pantone* marker

Hemlines

The hemlines of a design vary considerably from very simple hems to folds, pleats, gathers, fringing and beading, etc. The interest of the hemline may be featured on the hem of a skirt, sleeve or neckline.

The shape will vary from very full to narrow regular straight hems. Draped and shaped hems are often used on evening wear.

The hem is often trimmed with braids, tucks, frills and flounces.

A selection of hem lines on skirts producing different effects

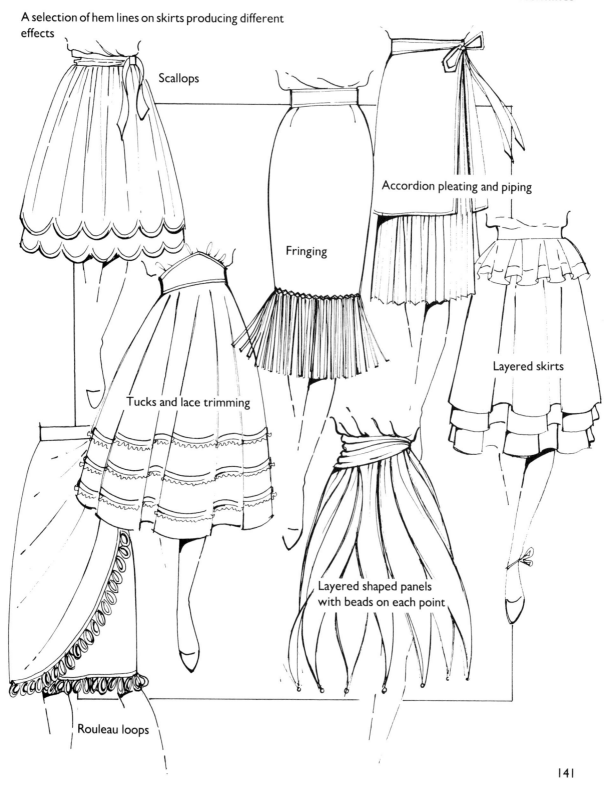

Scallops

Fringing

Accordion pleating and piping

Layered skirts

Tucks and lace trimming

Layered shaped panels with beads on each point

Rouleau loops

Hemlines

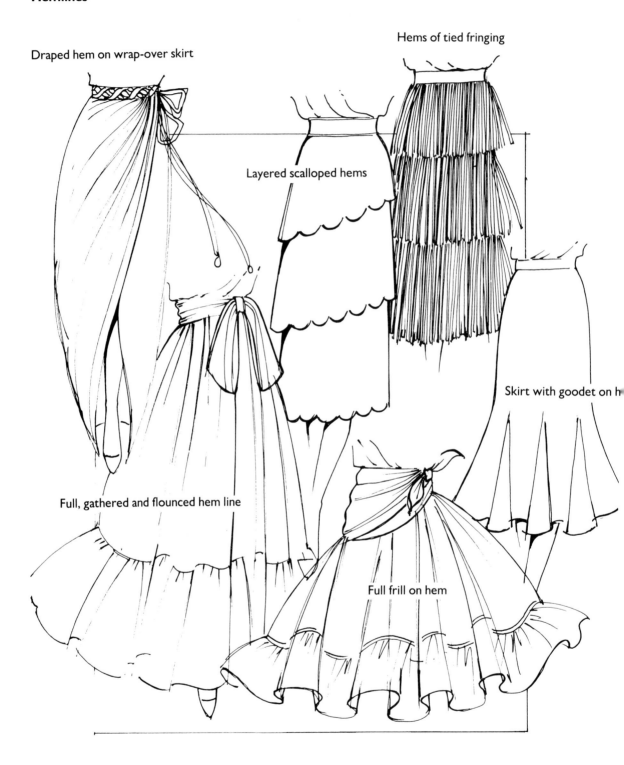

Draped hem on wrap-over skirt

Hems of tied fringing

Layered scalloped hems

Skirt with goodet on h

Full, gathered and flounced hem line

Full frill on hem

Short full cirtcular
skirt cut on the bias

Full length skirt cut on the bias

Skirts of soft folds at hem

Skirts illustrating different effects at the hemline
depending on the fabric used

Contrast fabric

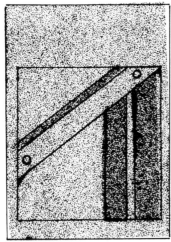
Leather insertions on a pocket

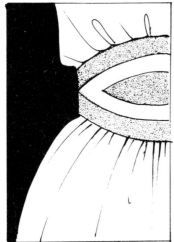
Contrast fabric on waist band

Insertions

This effect is achieved by stitching different sections of a contrasting material into a garment.

The contrast may be of a different colour, pattern or texture. The

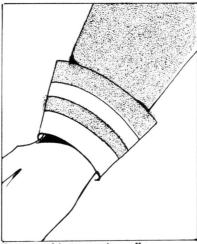
Contract fabrics on the cuff

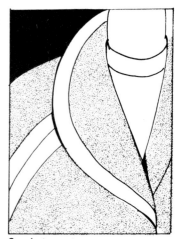
Suede insertions

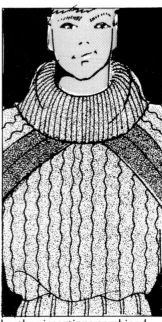
Leather insertions combined with a knitted texture

insertions will vary from knitted sections of ribing, leather, suede or lace to contrasting patterned fabric.

This effect is used in many areas of design from day and casual wear to very delicate designs made in lighter fabrics for day and evening wear as well as for lingerie.

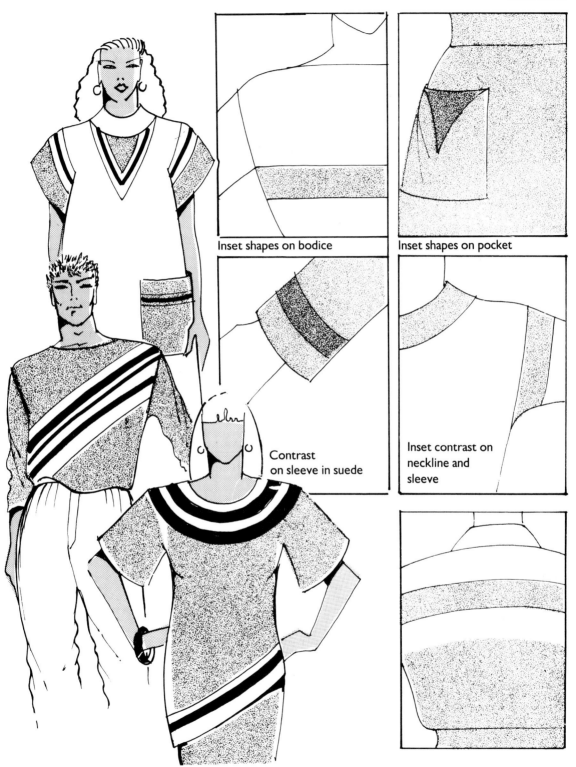

Inset shapes on bodice

Inset shapes on pocket

Contrast
on sleeve in suede

Inset contrast on
neckline and
sleeve

Piece of fabric inserted into garment
for decorative effect

Insertions

Contrast insets of leather combined with tweed fabrics

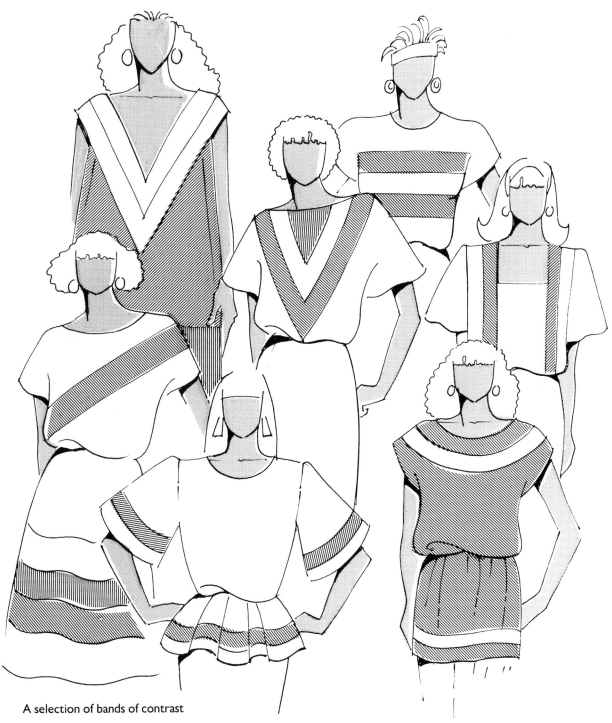

A selection of bands of contrast

Fabric inset on blouses, dresses, skirts and peplums

Jabot

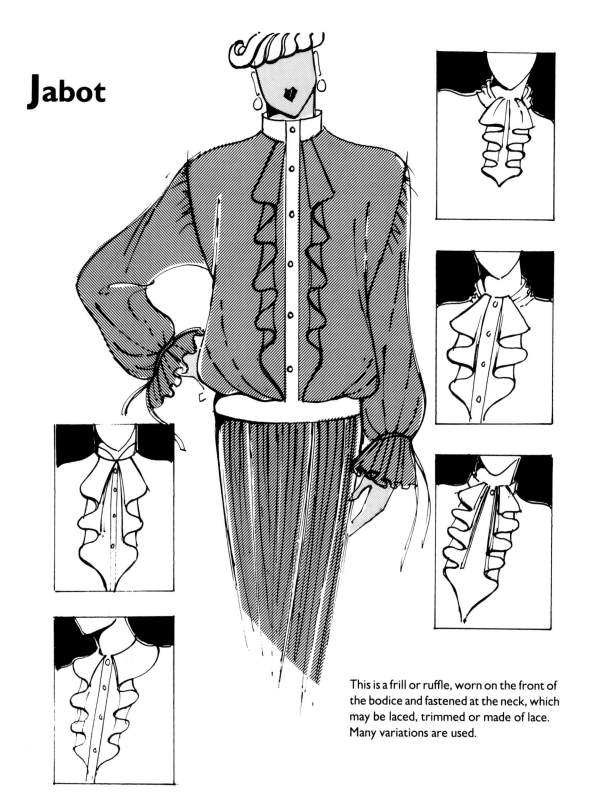

This is a frill or ruffle, worn on the front of the bodice and fastened at the neck, which may be laced, trimmed or made of lace. Many variations are used.

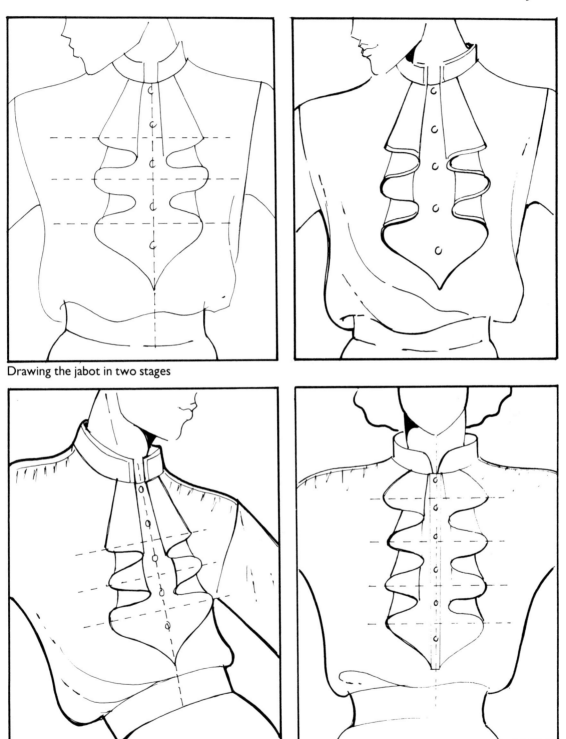

Drawing the jabot in two stages

Note the dotted line as a guide line when sketching

Knit

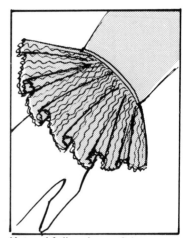

Knitted collar combined with tweed

Knitted frill on hem of sleeve

Inset

Knitted ribbed edging

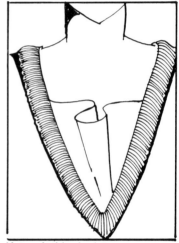

A large selection of yarns is available different colour mixtures and giving textured effects which can be incorporated as part of a design.

A knitted yoke, collar or inset section can add interest. The contrast of the texture of knitting combined with fabrics such as corduroy, tweeds, wool and light weight fabrics for evening wear combined with delicate yarns, look most attractive.

Knitted accessories such as hats, scarves and gloves can give a design a complete fashion image.

150

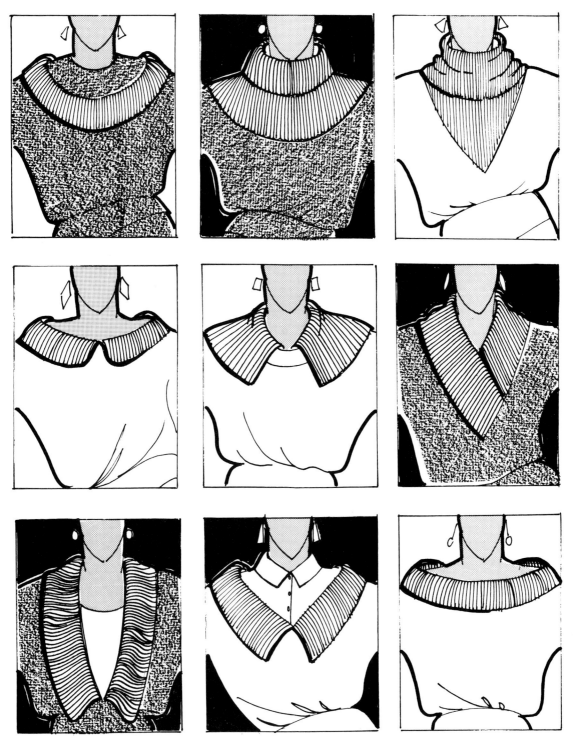

A selection of knitted ribbed collars

A selection of designs combining knitting yarns and fabric

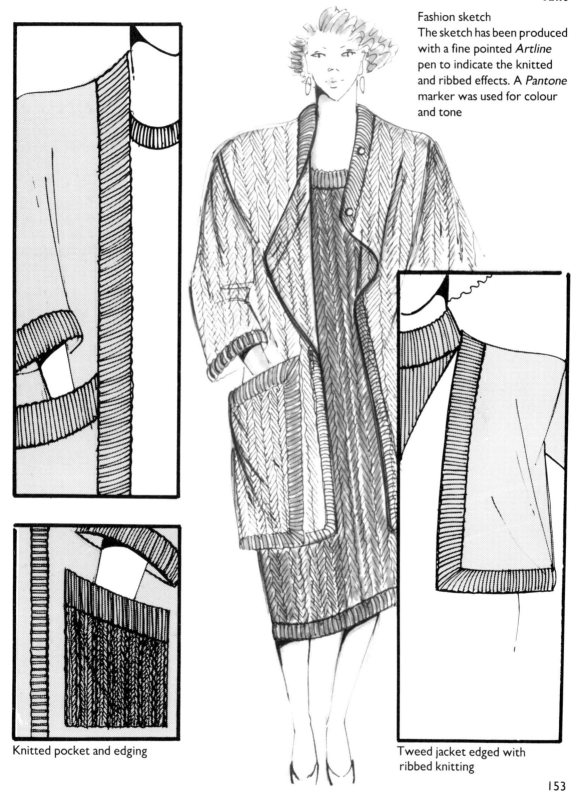

Fashion sketch
The sketch has been produced
with a fine pointed *Artline*
pen to indicate the knitted
and ribbed effects. A *Pantone*
marker was used for colour
and tone

Knitted pocket and edging

Tweed jacket edged with
ribbed knitting

Lacing

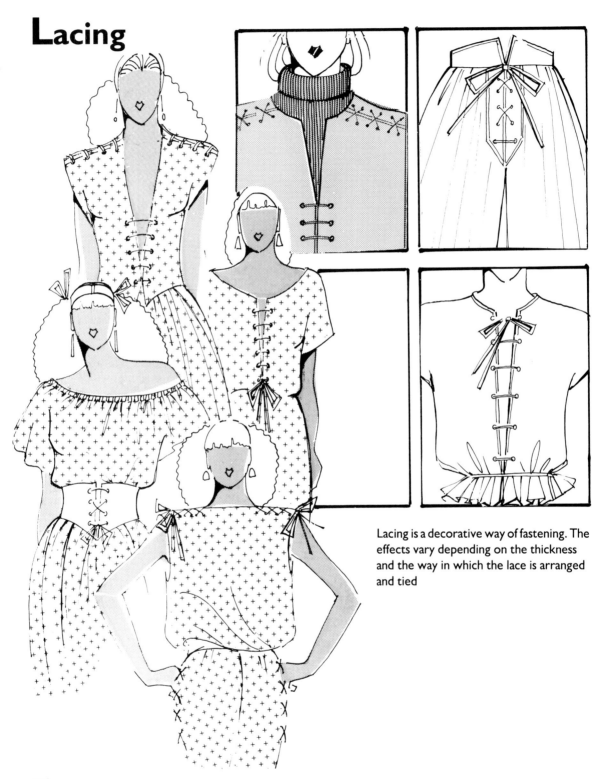

Lacing is a decorative way of fastening. The effects vary depending on the thickness and the way in which the lace is arranged and tied

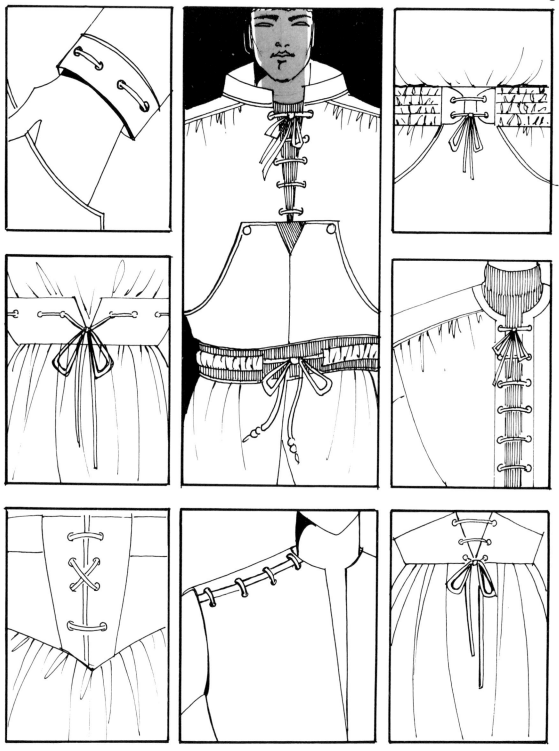

Macramé

Macramé is decorative knotting using two basic knots, the flat (or reef) and the half hitch, with variations. It produces a close firm texture which is hardwearing. The decorations will vary depending on the colours used and may be extended by making tassels or fringes, or by including beads in the design.

Fashion sketches
Combination of black paint
for dresses, with fine pen
work for macramé effects

Used as a fashion detail on a garment design

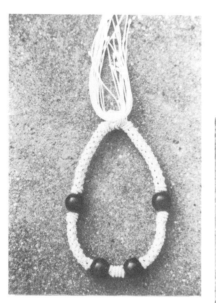

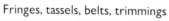
Fringes, tassels, belts, trimmings

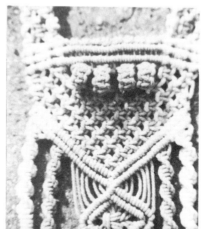

157

Necklines

Neckline shapes have many variations with a selection
of collars and trimmings from which to choose. Many
shapes and finishes are illustrated throughout the
book.

159

Necklines

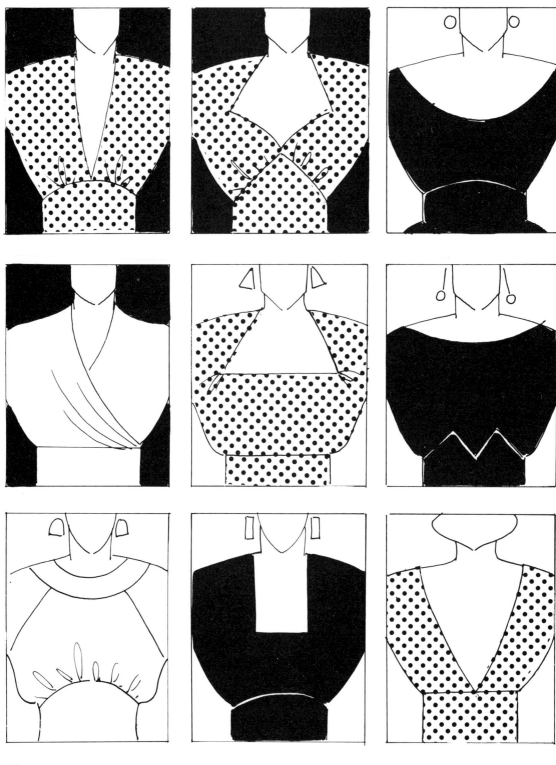

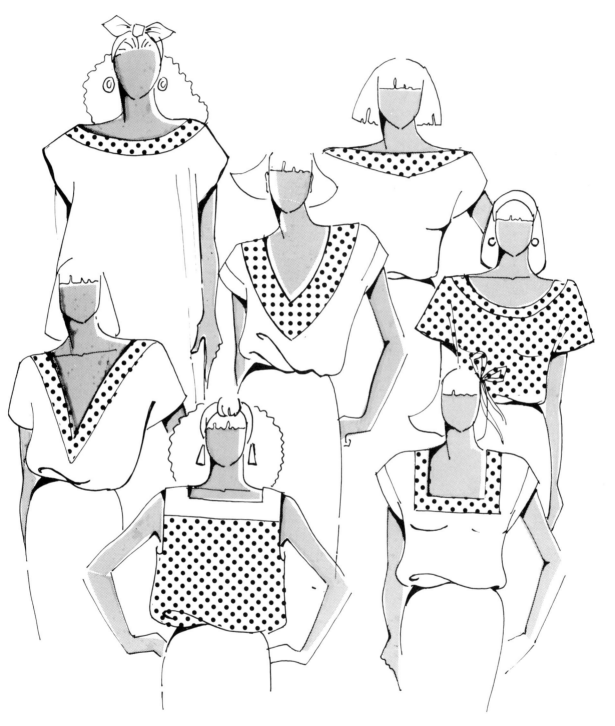

Necklines emphasised with contrasting fabrics

Necklines

A selection of finishes to the neckline

Patchwork

Whether you are designing a skirt, jacket or a dress the basic method is the same: simply joining one geometric shape of fabric to another edge to edge, stitched either by hand or by machine to create attractive effects on a border, collar and cuffs or for a complete garment.

Colour and pattern of the fabrics when designing the required effects of the fabrics selected must be of the same weight. If the fabrics vary too much the garment could lose its shape.

Individual and creative effects may be achieved when introducing patchwork in a design, depending on the variations of techniques used, eg padding individual patches or joining sections of patchwork together with embroidery stitches such as feather stitches, herringbone, coral and topstitching.

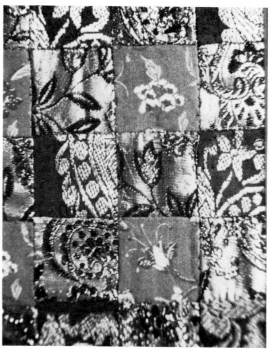

Patchwork square in rich brocades with a pattern in metallic threads

Cathedral window patchwork using spray dyed cotton

Log cabin patchwork using lino-printed cotton

Patchwork

Patchwork jacket with white contrast collar

Patchwork bolaro and peplum

Waistband and pocket

Cuff detail

Fashion sketch
A free line sketch produced with a drawing pen. A water-colour wash has been used for the tone effects of folds and face, arms and legs

Metallic printed silk, combining a number of patchwork techniques

Seminole patchwork produced with bright contrasting cotton, embellished with zigzag applied ribbon

Metallic printed leather squares joined with a metallic zigzag stitch to appear like traditional patchwork

Patchwork

Variations of patchwork

Variations of introducing patchwork on a design at
the neck, on a collar, cuff or a complete jacket dress
or skirt

Pleats

Stitched in place within the yoke

Knife pleats

Unpressed pleats

There are three basic pleats: knife, box and inverted. They are all folds of fabric and may be added to a design by allowing enough extra fabric where it is required an dfolding it into place.

Pleats give movement and are used in the design of a garment in a variety of ways on the skirt, bodice or sleeve. They may also be used as a style detail on a

pocket, within a yoke or panel. The pleat may be held at both ends or it may be held at one end and stitched in place for part of its length.

Unpressed pleats are held at one end but not stitched or pressed. The effects vary depend on the fabric and texture used from light sheer fabrics to wool and tweeds.

Knife pleats

Unpressed pleats

Knife pleats with a panel

Inverted pleat on pocket

Peplum of pleats

Box pleats from yoke line

Pleats

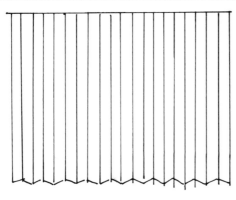

Accordion pleats

Often used on skirts, sleeves, collars and bodices. The fabric may be taken to a pleater to be treated. The depth of the pleat may vary according to the effect required and weight of the fabric used

A selection of accordion pleats used on a design, as a
collar, sleeve, peplum or skirt

Pleats

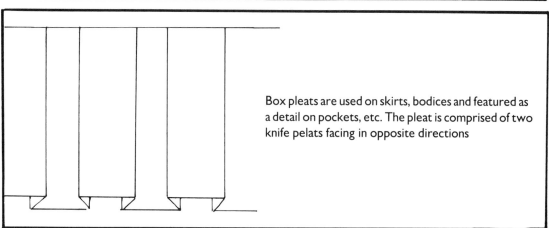

Box pleats are used on skirts, bodices and featured as a detail on pockets, etc. The pleat is comprised of two knife pelats facing in opposite directions

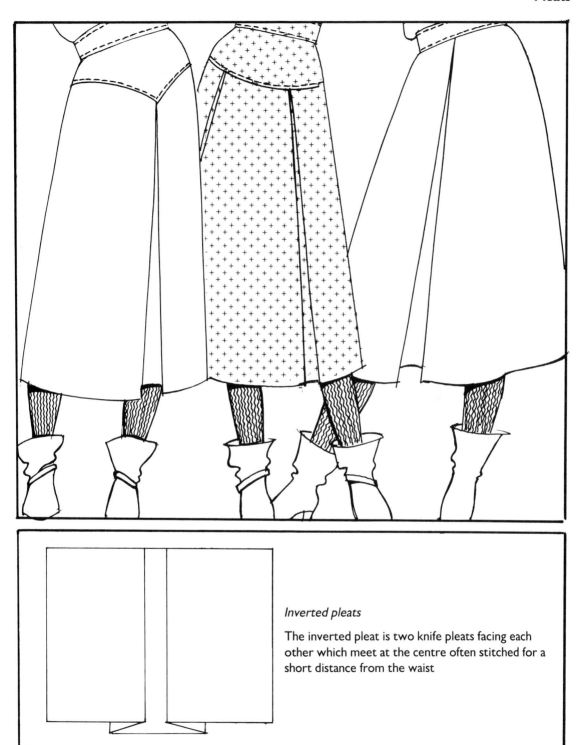

Inverted pleats

The inverted pleat is two knife pleats facing each other which meet at the centre often stitched for a short distance from the waist

Pleats

Inverted pleats

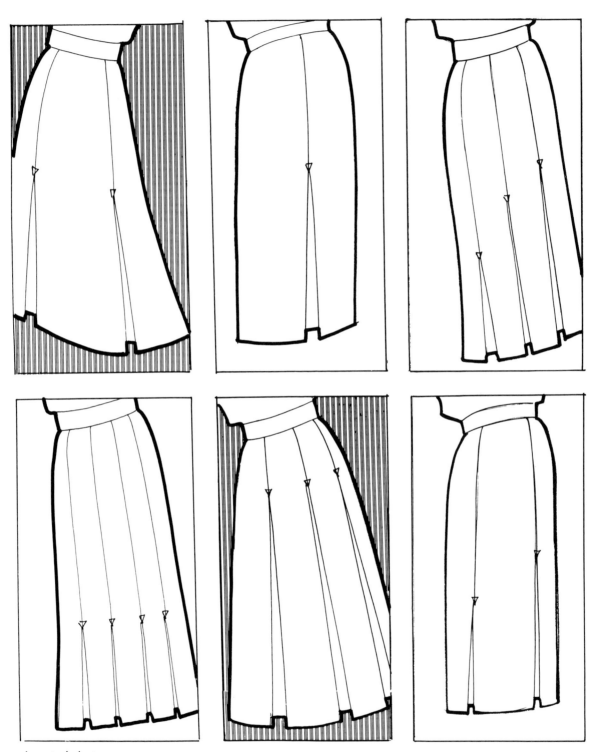

Inverted pleats

Pleats

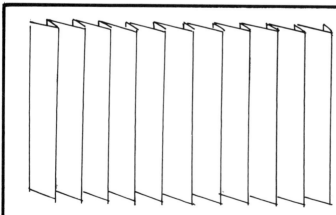

Knife pleats

The knife pleat is a simple fold in the fabric pressed to one side. The pleats may be arranged in different ways; continuously on a skirt, in groups, or as single pleats (as illustrated)

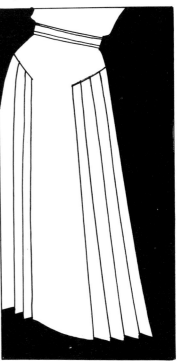

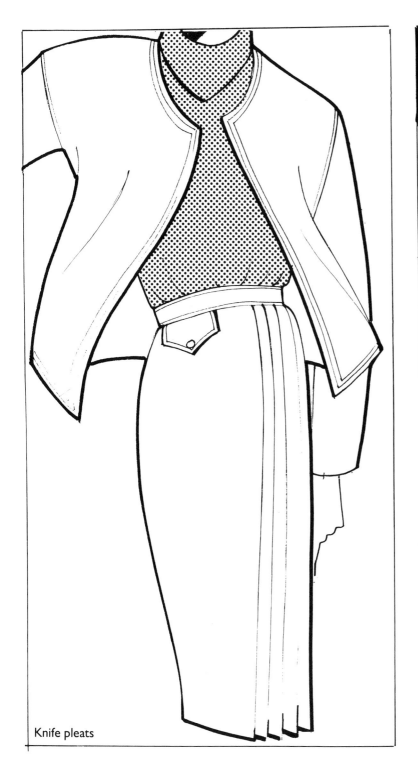

Knife pleats

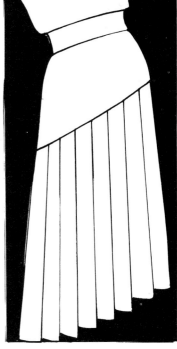

Pleats

Knife pleats on skirts in a selection of different arrangements

Pleats
gathered
from the yoke

Accordion pleated collar

Pleats held at
both ends
within the
yoke

Knife pleats stitched into cuff

Pleats inset into panel

Anchored knife pleats

Pleat held at both ends and stitched in place for part of its length

Pleats

Fashion sketch
The effect of movement of a
light thin fabric with crystal
pleating has been achieved
with a very fine *Artline* pen. A
colour wash has been added
to the face, arms and legs

Crystal pleats

These are fine accordion pleats up to
3 mm (¹/₈ in.) in width

185

Pockets

Patch pockets   In seam pockets   Front hip pocket   Slashed pockets with welts

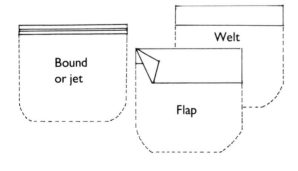

Bound or jet

Welt

Flap

Pockets may be made up first and then stitched onto the outside of the garment or they may be made as part of the garment and concealed within it.

The pocket may be used as a decorative feature on a design often with added details, eg pleats, gathers, seams, etc.

Flap pockets are produced as a slit in the fabric. They may vary in size and position, may be cut horizontal, vertical or curved

There are three ways of finishing a slit pocket. *Bound* which looks like a bound button hole. The *flap* which is inserted into the upper edge of the slash. *Welt* which is a separate piece of fabric sewn into the lower edge of the slit

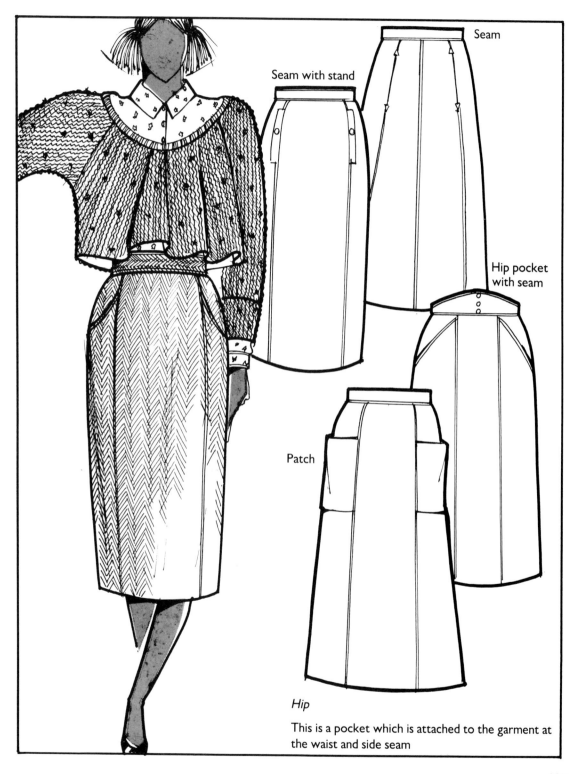

Seam

Seam with stand

Hip pocket
with seam

Patch

Hip

This is a pocket which is attached to the garment at
the waist and side seam

Pockets

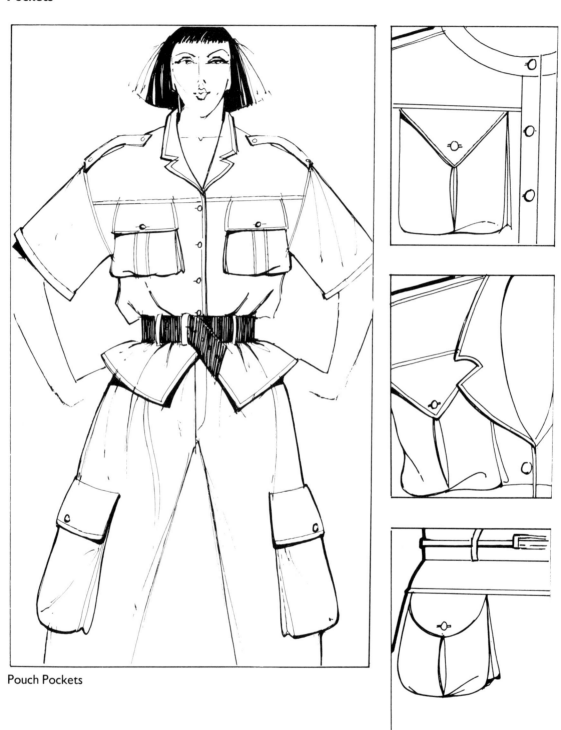

Pouch Pockets

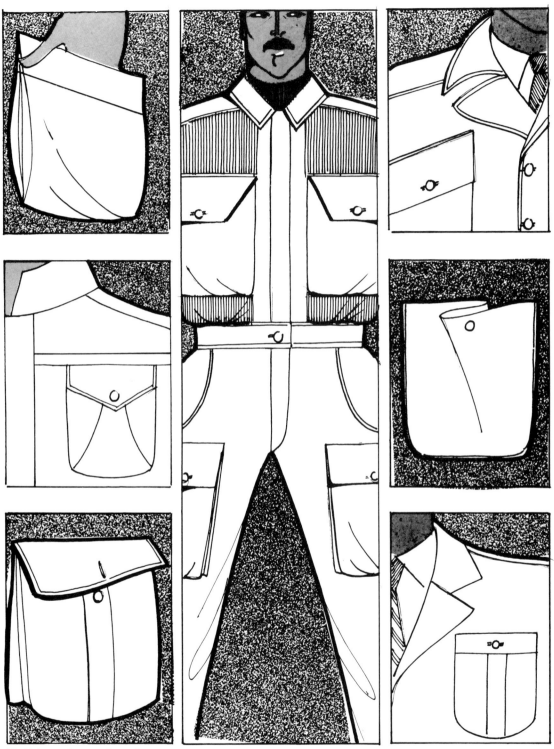

Variations of a pouch pocket

Pockets

Stylized fashion sketch produced
with a *Rotring* pen. A felt tip pen
was used for the hair

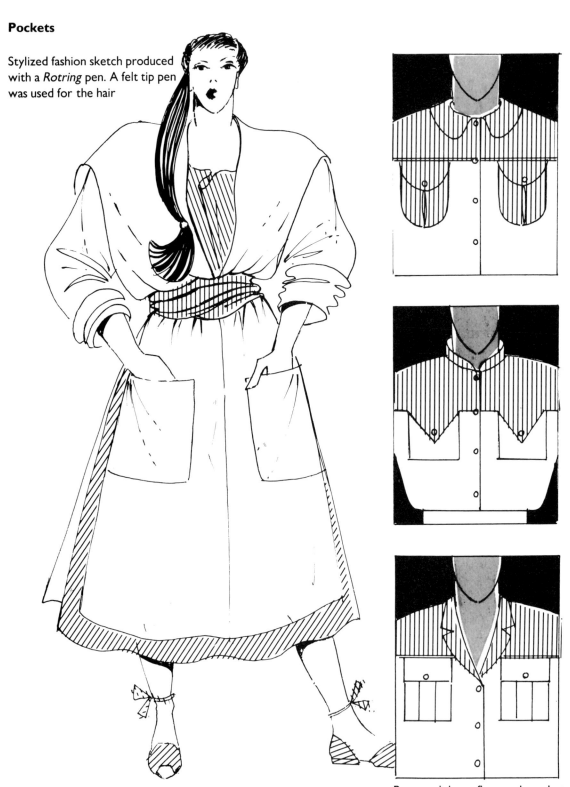

Buttoned down flap patch pockets
in contrast fabrics combined with
the yoke

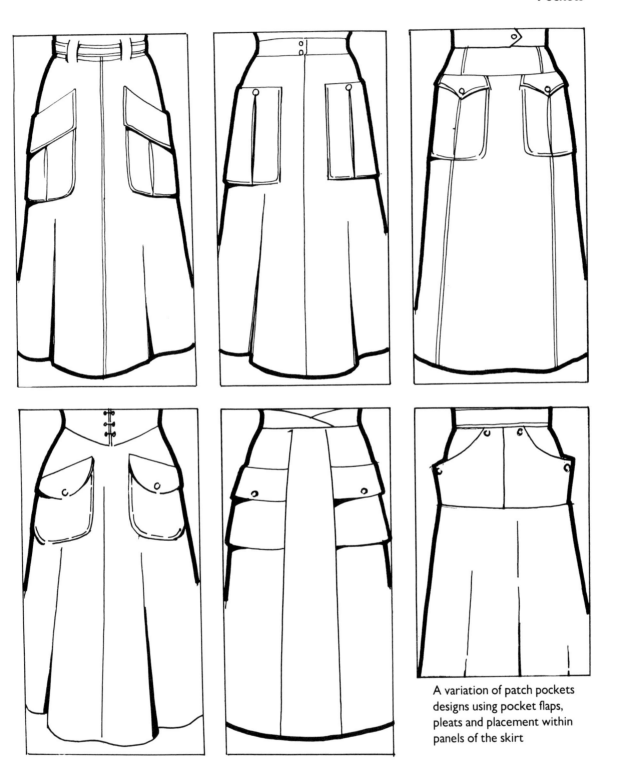

A variation of patch pockets
designs using pocket flaps,
pleats and placement within
panels of the skirt

191

Pockets

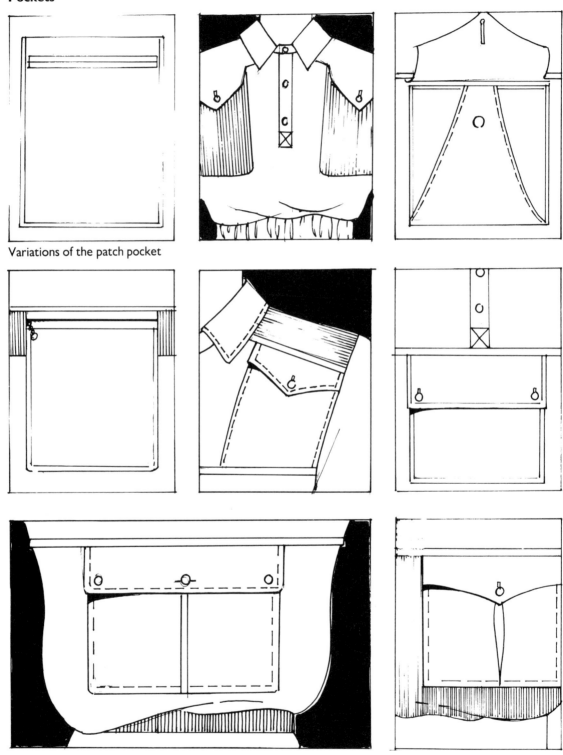

Variations of the patch pocket

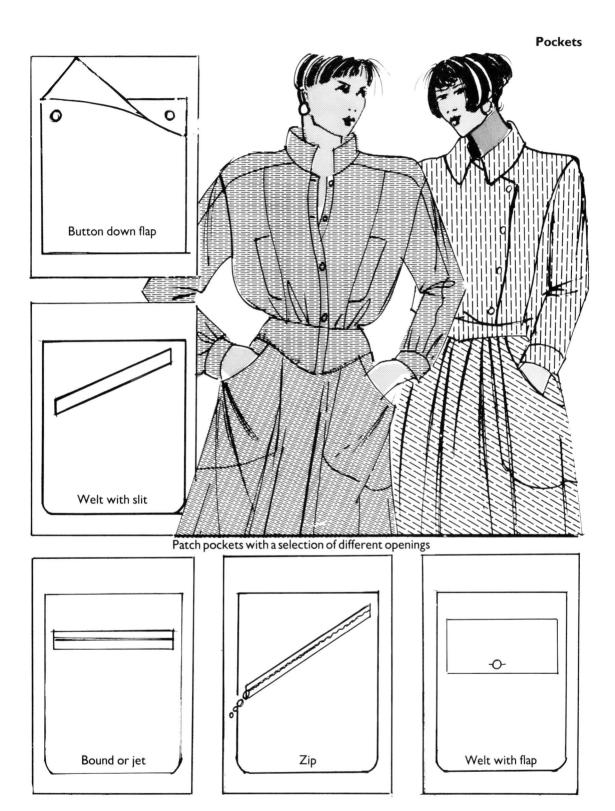

Button down flap

Welt with slit

Patch pockets with a selection of different openings

Bound or jet

Zip

Welt with flap

Pockets

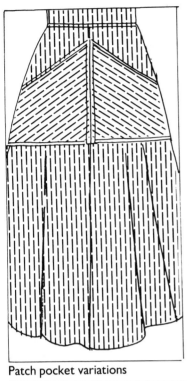 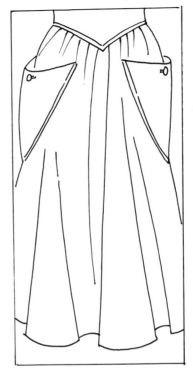 

Patch pocket variations

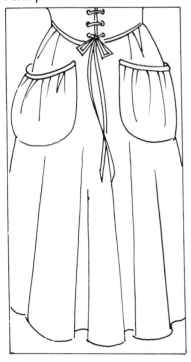 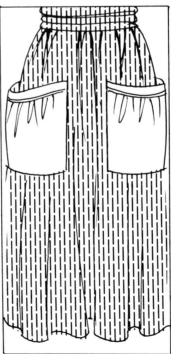 

Patch pocket

The pocket is placed on the outside of the garment

Pockets

Hip pockets

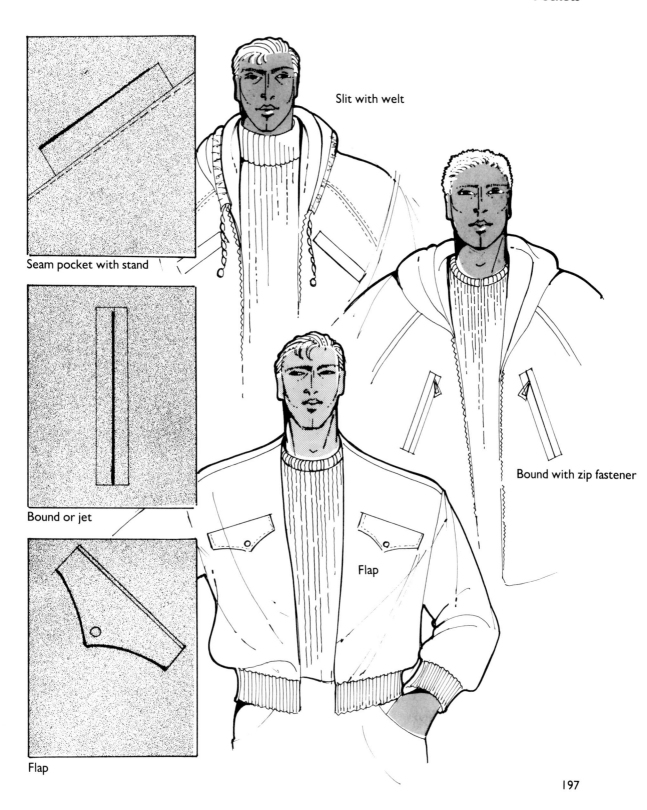

Seam pocket with stand

Bound or jet

Flap

Slit with welt

Bound with zip fastener

Flap

Flap

Quilting

The techniques of quilting vary depending on the effects required. The basic method is of joining three layers of fabric together with stitching, using linear or circular patterns.

Raised quilting

A decorative method padding certain areas of a design.

Cord quilting

The cord is sharply raised from the fabric to define the pattern.

Trupunto quilting

This is a padded form of raised quilting which can be used on its own or combined with wadded and cord quilting.

Potato printed cotton with hand quilting

Shadow quilting: two layers of silk organza sandwiching coloured wools

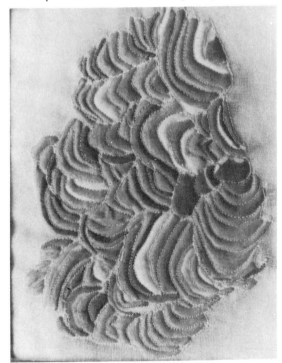

Shadow quilting: two layers of silk organza sandwiching coloured wools

Quilting

Fashion sketch
Stylized sketch
using a wax
crayon for
sections of
quilting working
over a textured
surface.

The detail has
been added with a
black fine pointed
pencil, tone added
on face and hands

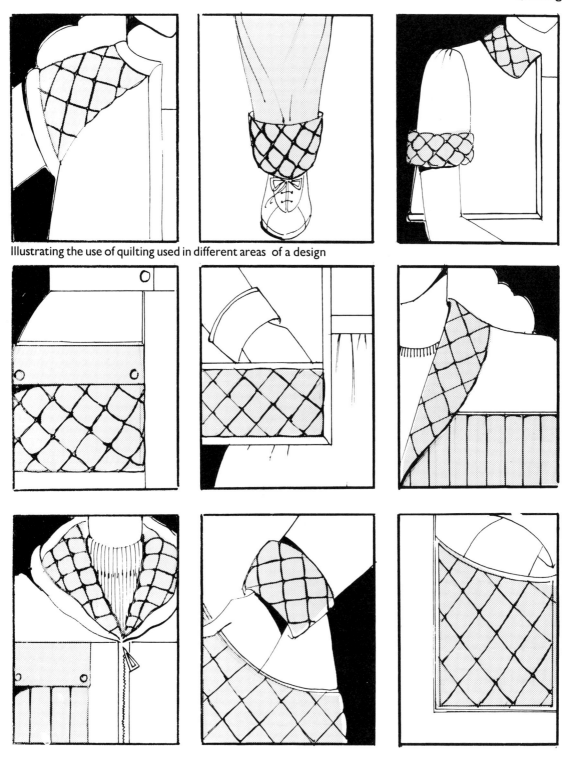

Illustrating the use of quilting used in different areas of a design

Quilting

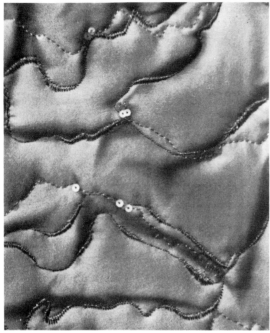

Spray dyed silk satin, quilting with straight and satin stitch, with tambour beading

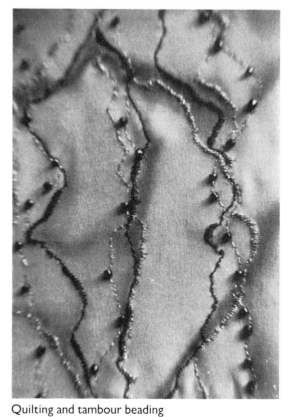

Quilting and tambour beading

English quilting with couching and french knots

Fashion sketches
Line drawings produced with a fine pointed pen.
The quilting effects have been suggested with
water-colour washes

Spray dyed silk satin with machine
quilting

Rouleau

This is a roll or fold of fabric cut on the bias used for piping and decorative effects.

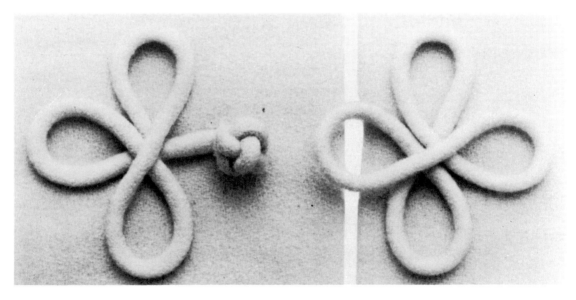

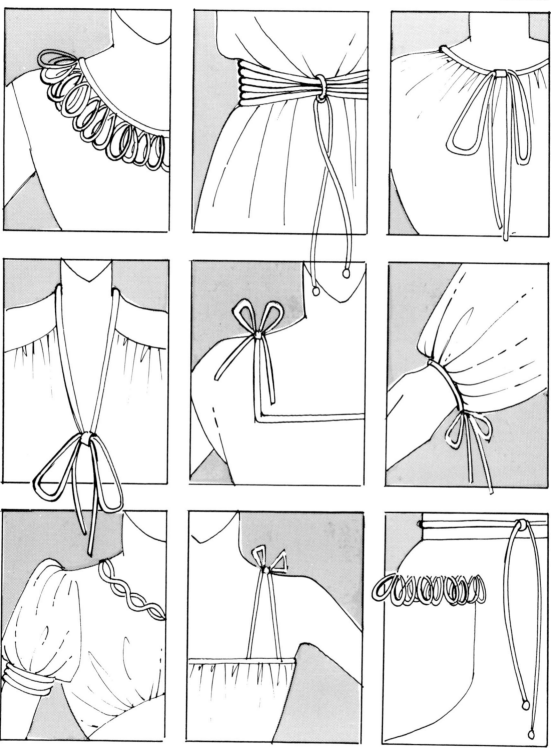

Seams

Fashion sketch
The sketch is produced with a thick black
pencil. Finer details added with a sharp
pointed pencil

Seams produce style lines in a design creating shape
and often a decorative effect. Many seam techniques
are featured in a design, eg piped, contrasting slot
seams, ruched, top stitching, etc.

Other seams are selected for their strength such as
when designing garments for sports and casual wear
or for their suitability for particular fabrics.

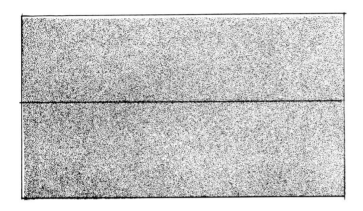

Plain seam

This is a line of stitching, produced by hand or machine to hold two pieces of fabric together. The different seams are selected for being decorative as well as functional.

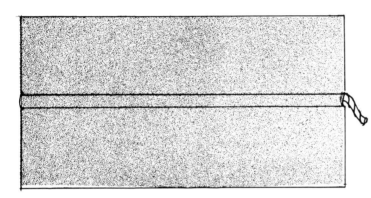

Corded or piped seam

The cord is covered by a bias cut strip of fabric. The piping cord is made of cotton which may be purchased in a variety of thickness and may match or be contrasting to the fabric of the garment.

This effect of piped seams is often used on designs when emphasising seam placement.

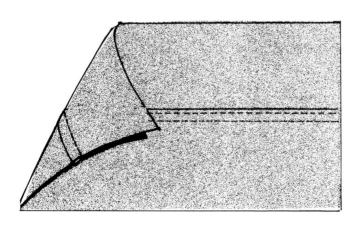

Flat felled seam

A strong neat seam which may be made to appear on the inside or on the outside of a garment. It looks most effective when used on the outside as a feature on casual and sports wear.

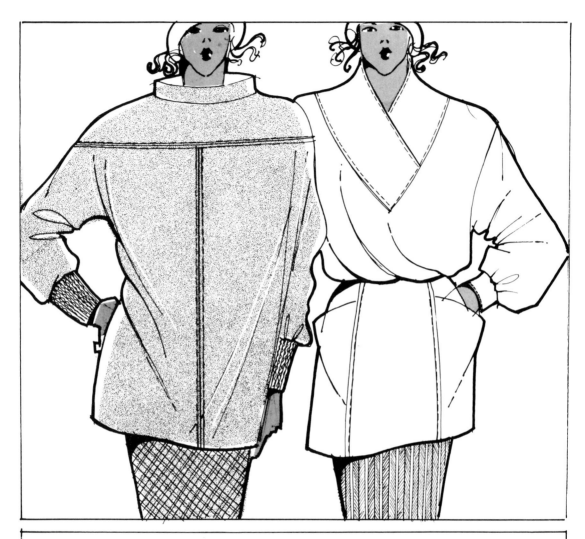

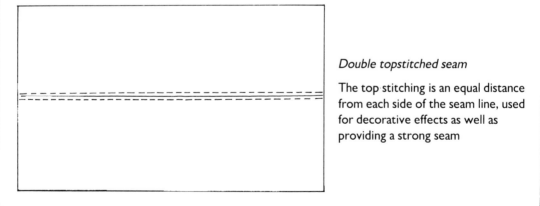

Double topstitched seam

The top stitching is an equal distance from each side of the seam line, used for decorative effects as well as providing a strong seam

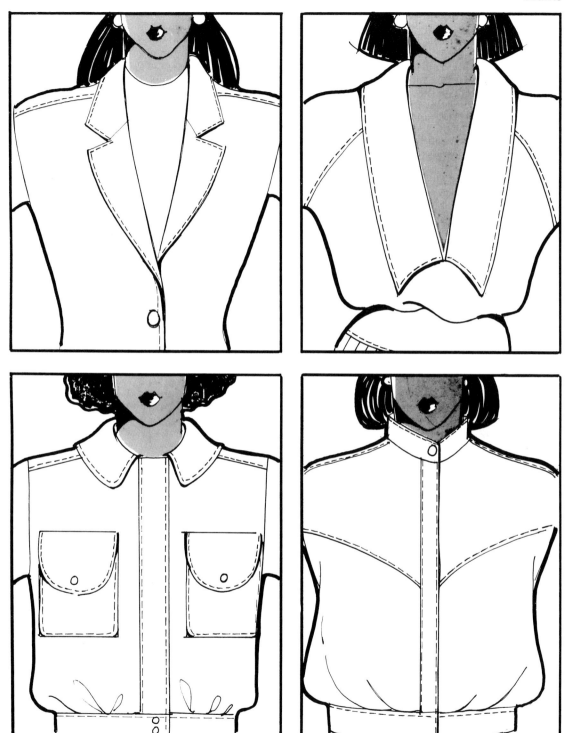

Single topstitched seam

Provides a decorative effect emphasising the shape of a collar, cuff, yoke or pocket. A contrast thread may also be used

209

Seams

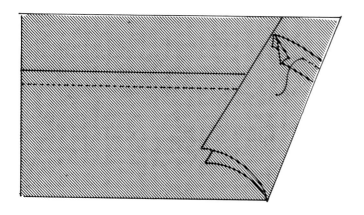

Welt seam

A variation of the felled seam, this seam is used on heavier fabrics for extra strength often on children's casual wear, industrial garments and sports wear.

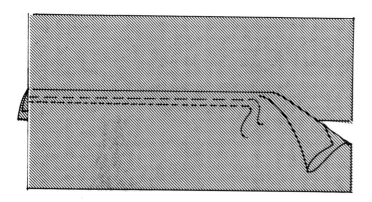

Tucked seam

This is attractive as a decorative feature, but not suitable for thick fabric.

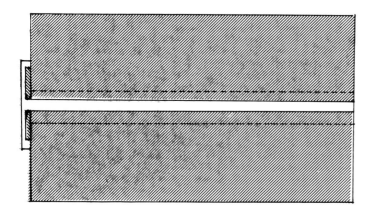

Slot seam

A decorative seam adding interest with a contrasting fabric placed underneath the seam. The detail can be introduced on yokes, sleeves, cuffs, waistbands, pockets and panel seams. It can be made with a plain fabric, cut on the bias, or with a contrasting pattern.

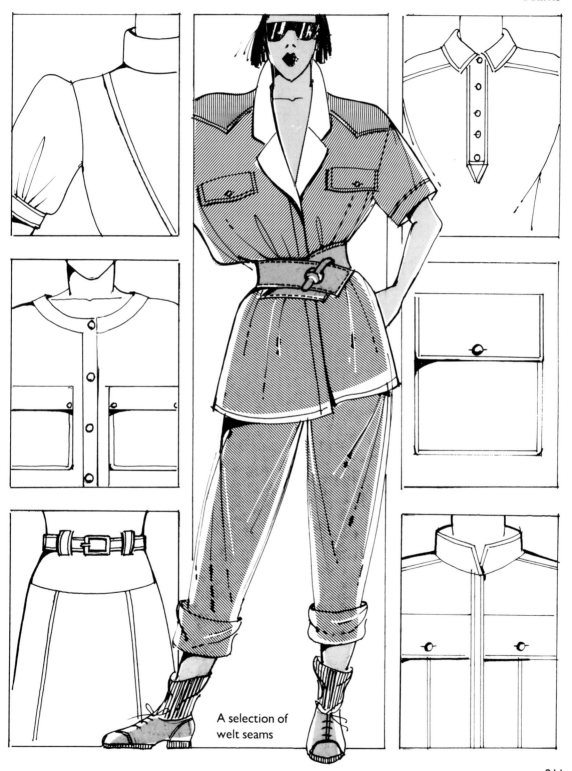

A selection of welt seams

Seams

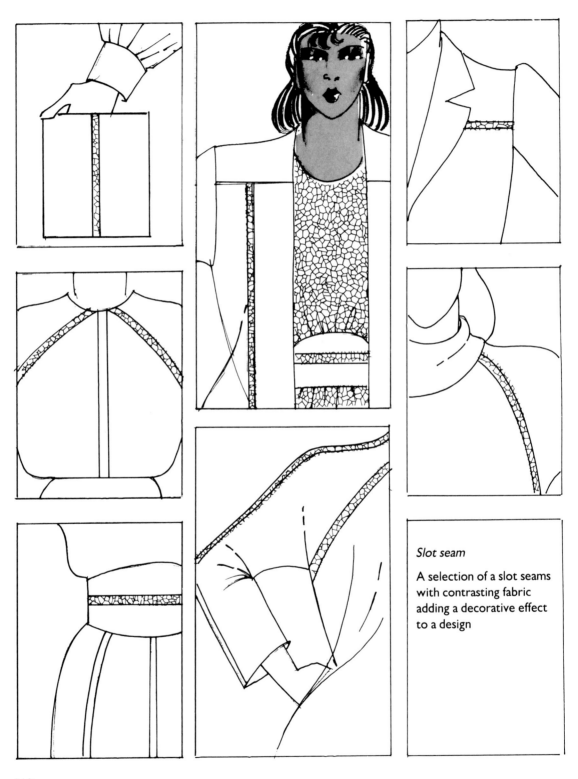

Slot seam

A selection of a slot seams with contrasting fabric adding a decorative effect to a design

Overlaid seam

One piece of fabric is laid over the other and stitched from the right side. The advantages of this seam are that the fabric always has the right side uppermost; it may be used on seams of any shape, it is also easier when arranging gathers from a seam, enabling one to achieve the effects required by moving the gathers if necessary.

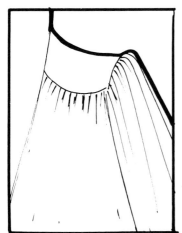

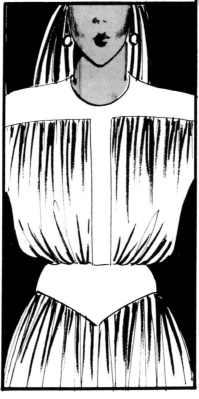

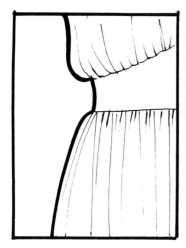

Gathered seam

This is a very decorative, the fullness being gathered into a seam. The effect will vary depending on the fabric and amount of gathers used. This detail is often used on sleeves, cuffs, yokes and waistbands.

A selection of gathered effects in the detail of a design, suggesting a soft fabric gathered into small folds, ie jersey, silk, voile or fine velvet.

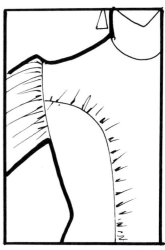

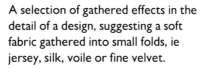

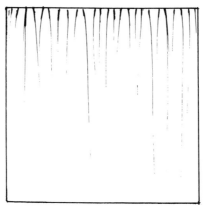

Top stitching as a decorative feature, emphasising
seam detail

Seams

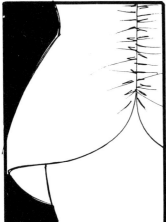

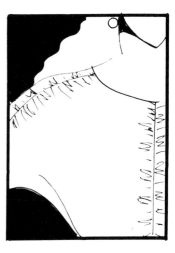

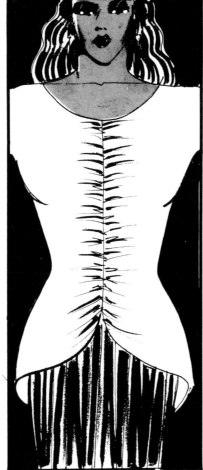

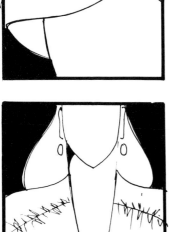

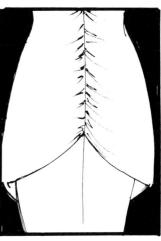

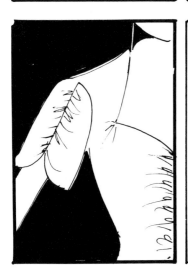

Ruched seam

This seam gives a very decorative effect used on the skirt, sleeve, bodice or shoulders. The seam is drawn up to achieve the effect of ruching

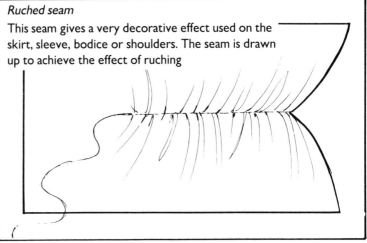

Variations of the ruched seam in a design

Shirring

Rows of shirring elastic are used to provide a
decorative way of controlling fullness over a wide
area. The stretchy effect of shirring hugs the body and
expands with the body movements. It may be used
for the entire bodice of a garment or for just a small
section on the cuff, shoulder or hips. Lightweight
fabrics are the most suitable.

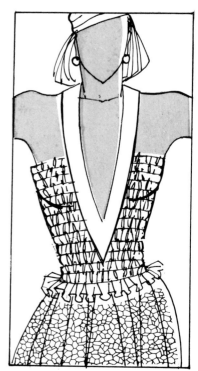

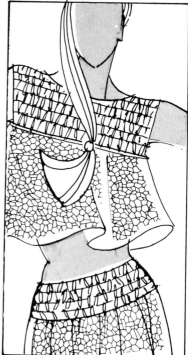

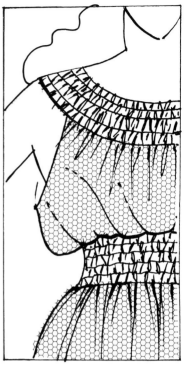

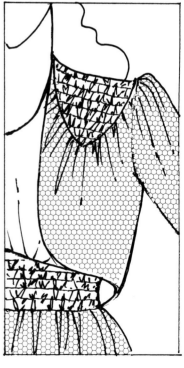

Shirring

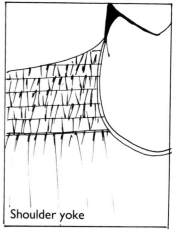

Shoulder yoke

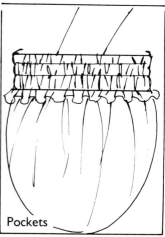

Pockets

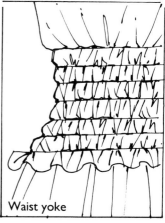

Waist yoke

Waistband

Sleeve cuff

Shoulder
straps
and
bodice

Sleeves

There are many variations of the sleeve but they are based on three main styles: set-in, raglan and kimono. A wide selection of sleeves is illustrated throughout the book. Note the many effects achieved by adding cuffs, gathers, pleats, tucks and variations of the cutting of a sleeve from tight fitting sleeves to very full ones.

The fabrics used give a variety of different effects to the design from the soft, flowing fabrics to the more heavy rich and textured brocades.

Dropped shoulders with set-in sleeve

Basic styles from which many variations may be designed

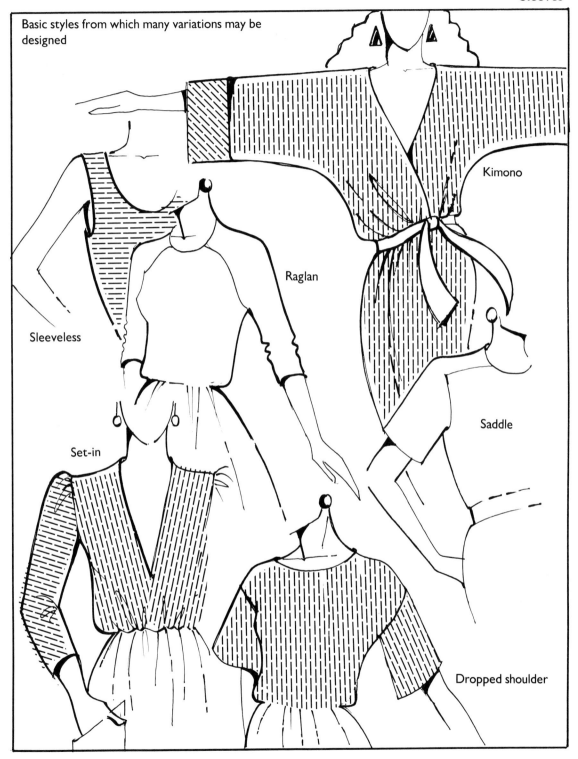

Kimono

Raglan

Sleeveless

Saddle

Set-in

Dropped shoulder

223

Sleeves

Bishop sleeve

Large puff sleeve

Three-quarter length sleeve

Set-in sleeve

This sleeve is set into the arm hole shape of the bodice. The sleeve has variations with gathers at the sleeve head or is slightly rounded. The styles may vary being large and full in shape with variations of length, or be cut, gathered, pleated and have cuff interest

Decoration may also be applied

A selection of set-in sleeves with gathers at the sleeve head and cuff. Note the variation of armhole shapes and fullness of the sleeve

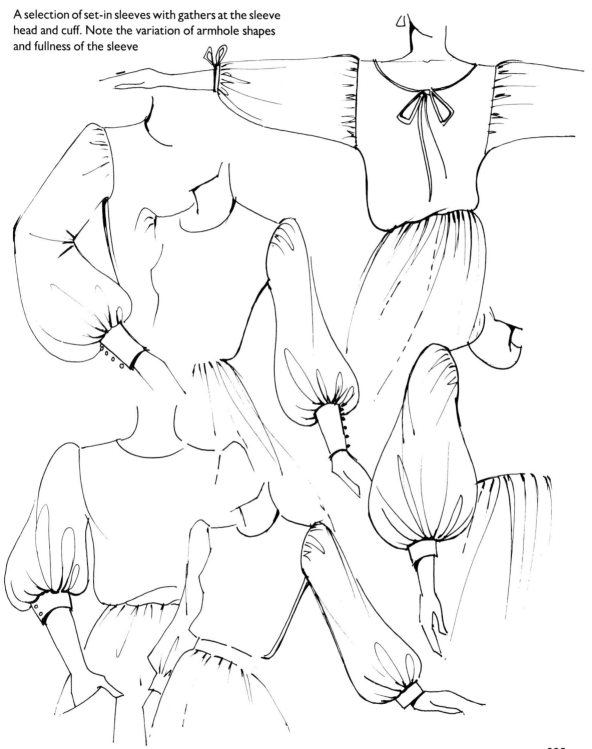

Sleeves

Kimono sleeve

Variations of a kimono cut sleeve

Sleeves

Raglan sleeve

Variations of the raglan sleeve

Sleeves

Saddle sleeve

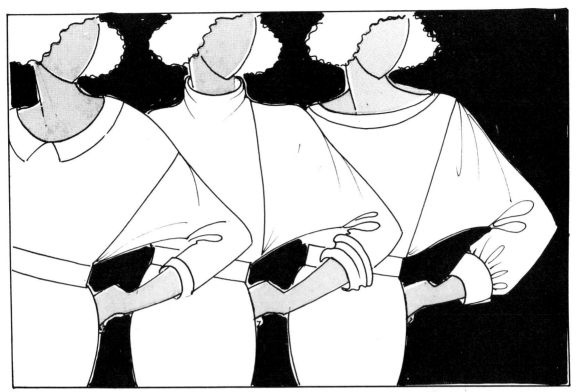

Bat wing variations

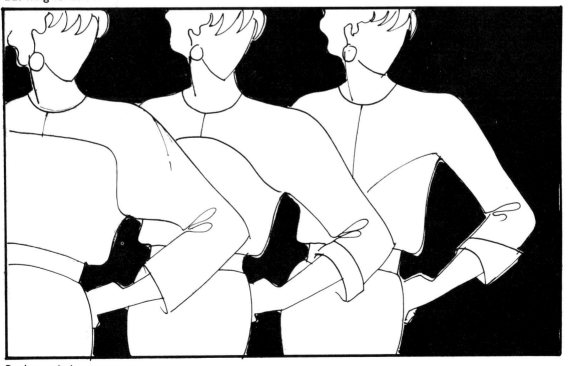

Raglan variations

Sleeves

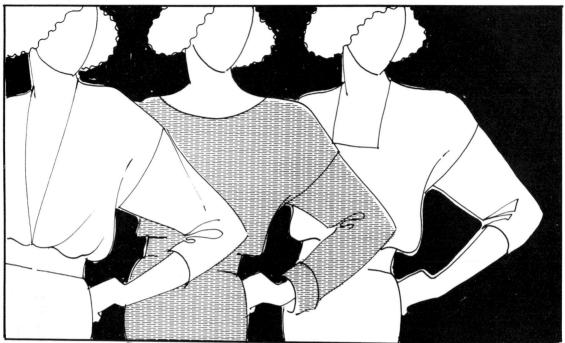

Dropped shoulder

Set-in sleeve

232

A selection of styles

Saddle

Raglan

Set-in, puff

Kimono

Smocking

Smocking using traditional embroidery stitches

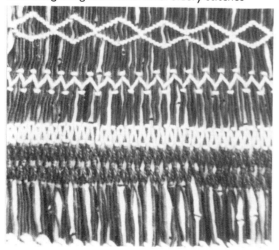

Smocking may be worked on many fabrics from printed cottons and ginghams to silks, lightweight woollen fabrics and tweeds. It is a very effective decoration used on many designs from children's garments today and evening wear.

Smocking is achieved with embroidery yarns which would be selected according to the type of fabric used. It can also be introduced to give a textured effect using fabric and yarns in the same colour, or every row of smocking may be produced in a different colour or in a variety of colours.

Once the gathering has been done, there is a large selection of embroidery stitches from which to form the pattern, depending on the effects required.

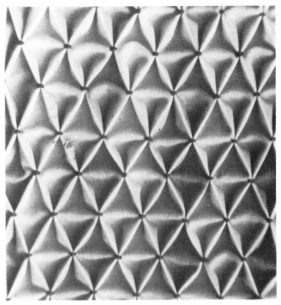

Mock smocking using
honeycomb stitch

Free machining over the flutes of
tightly gathered smocking

Smocking

Smocking placed in different areas of a design

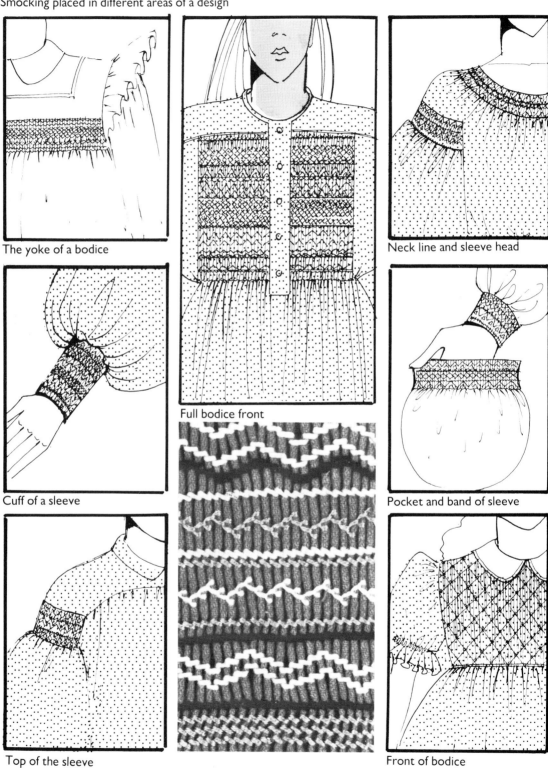

The yoke of a bodice

Full bodice front

Neck line and sleeve head

Cuff of a sleeve

Pocket and band of sleeve

Top of the sleeve

Front of bodice

Free machine embroidery on the flutes of the smocking with applied net

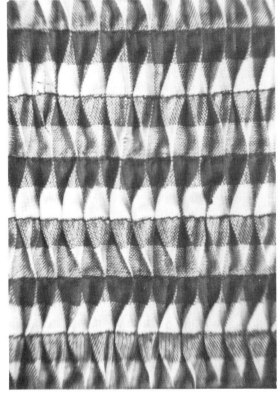

Counterchange smocking on gingham

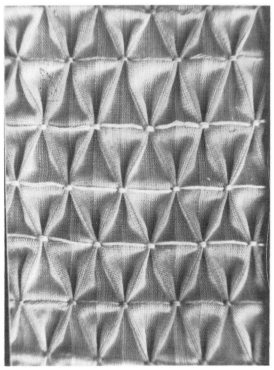

Mock smocking using the reverse side of honeycombe stitch

Tassels

These may be made from a selection of different materials. The designs vary from small single effects to elaborate designs often used as a main feature on a garment.

Photographed are a number of different styles showing the imaginative use of materials from beading to macramé.

Ties

The tie has many variations depending on the size, cut and material used. The style may be very full or narrow, softly draped or have a crisp neat look. It is used as a decorative detail and may also serve as a fastener. It can be used on different areas of a garment design.

Tucks

A tuck is a fold of fabric used as a decorative feature, holding fullness and used for shaping. They are even in width and stitched in groups or arranged on a complete section of a garment. The effects vary depending on the thickness of the fabric texture and pattern. They are more attractive when used on fine delicate fabrics.

The following sketches illustrate different ways in which they may be used and methods of suggesting the effects of a tuck on a design.

Tucks

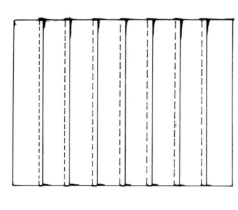

Pin tucks

The tucks are very fine and narrow and they should be very close together; they cannot be pressed to one side so tend to stand up. They are often combined with embroidery and lace and look effective when used in a panel or on a pocket or yoke

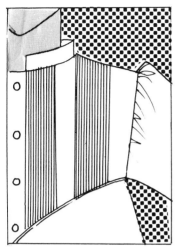

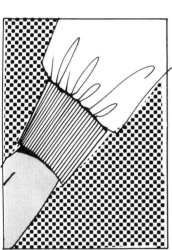

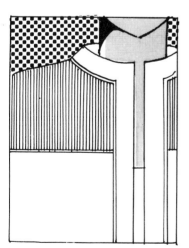

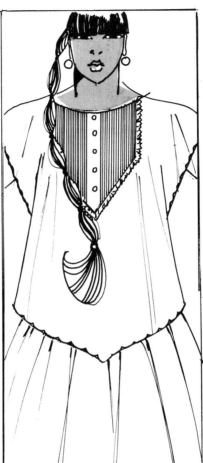

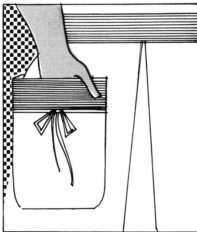

Tucks in groups

Tucks arranged on pockets, cuffs, bodices, yokes and sleeves
Pin tucks

Groups of small pin tucks placed within sections of a design. The sectons are edged with piping or lace

Tucks

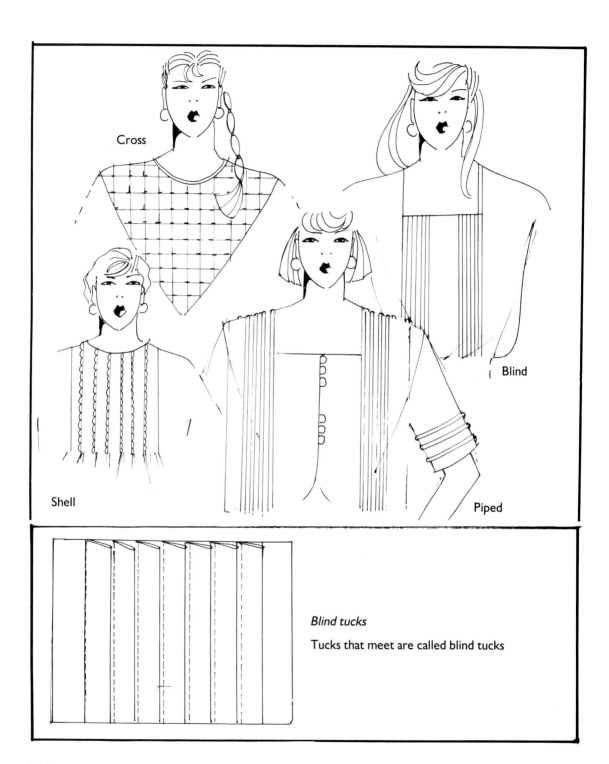

Cross

Blind

Shell

Piped

Blind tucks

Tucks that meet are called blind tucks

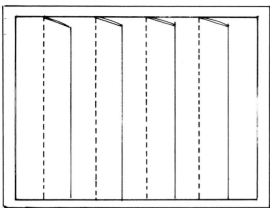

Spaced tucks

The spaced tuck has an even amount of space between each one

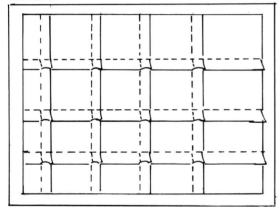

Cross tucks

The cross tuck gives a very pleasing effect when used on yokes, pockets and large areas of a garment

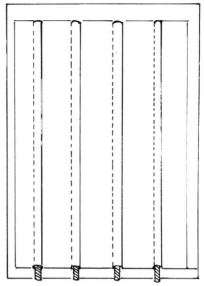

Piped tucks

Piped tucks are used to effect on design to emphasise the tuck. Piping cord is inserted into each tuck

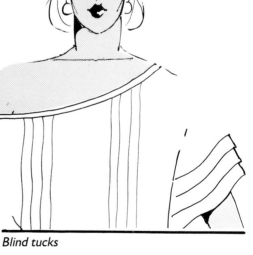

Blind tucks

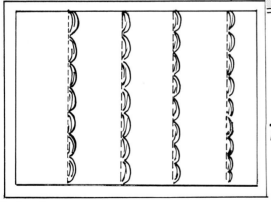

Shell tucks

The shell tuck gives a very attractive scalloped edge to a tuck. The effect is often used on delicate fabrics for evening wear and children's designs

245

Tucks

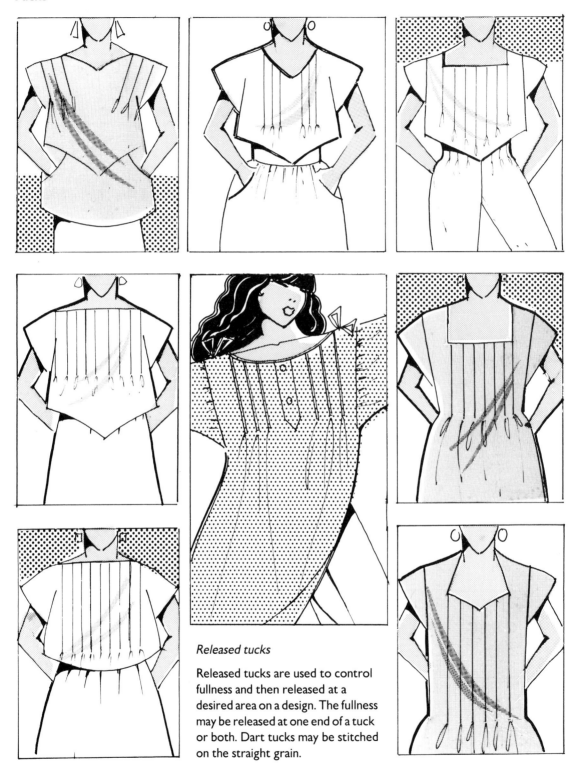

Released tucks

Released tucks are used to control fullness and then released at a desired area on a design. The fullness may be released at one end of a tuck or both. Dart tucks may be stitched on the straight grain.

Underskirts

Gathers and piping

Inset lace section

Tucks and lace

Layered frills

Underskirts may be an important feature to give emphasis to the skirt shape and fullness, also when featured as a layered look draped to be revealed below the skirt.

The hem line is often the feature of an underskirt with different effects of gathering, pleating, frills and flounces.

Scallops and
gathers

Lace inset
and
accordion
pleating

Blind tucks

Gathered hem line

Vents and Slits

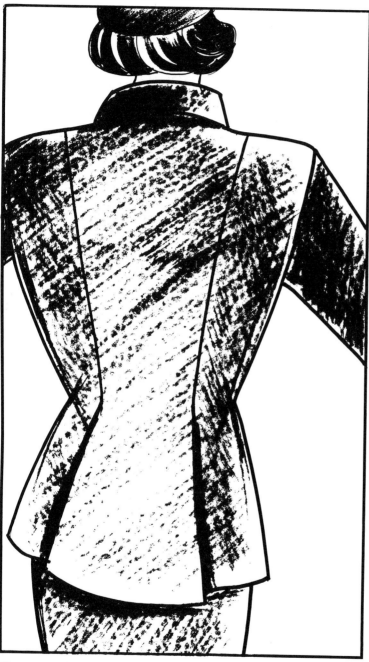

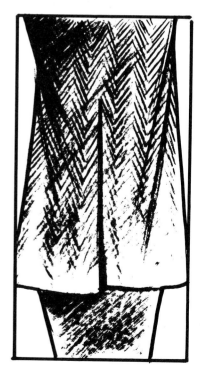

These provide an opening which differs in length:
often used on a jacket, maybe in the centre back or at
the sides. Technically a vent is a slit which overlaps
another piece of fabric.

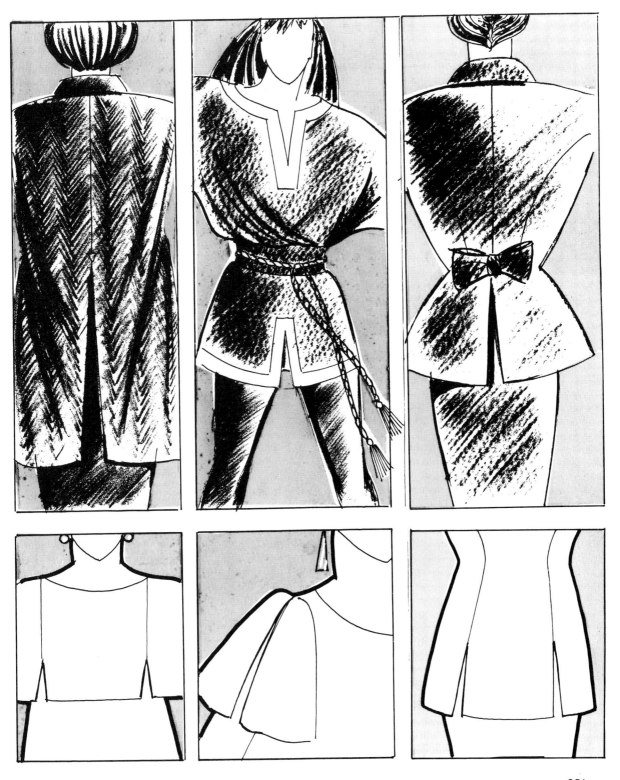

Waistbands

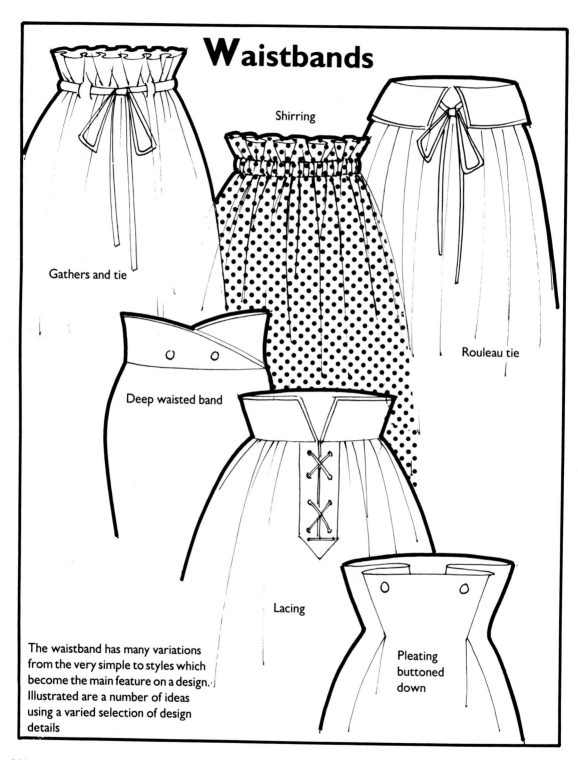

Shirring

Gathers and tie

Rouleau tie

Deep waisted band

Lacing

Pleating buttoned down

The waistband has many variations from the very simple to styles which become the main feature on a design. Illustrated are a number of ideas using a varied selection of design details

Waistband shapes with style features

Waistbands

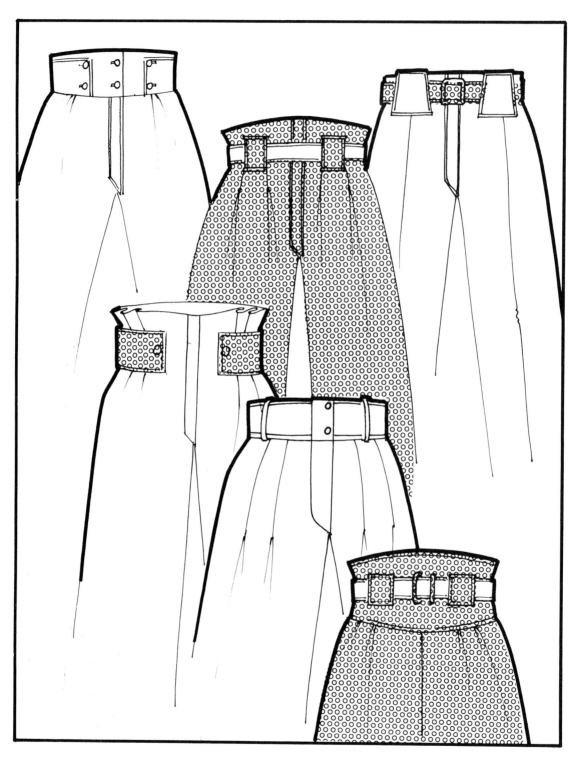

Yokes

The yoke is a flat area of a garment. It is often in contrasting material, piped to emphasise the shape or it may incorporate quilting, embroidery, pleating, tucks, appliqué or decorative stitching.

The yoke is placed on a garment to add to the design and can produce a variety of shapes based on curves and squares.

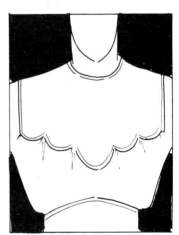

Yokes with scallops and gathers placed on the bodice
of a blouse or dress

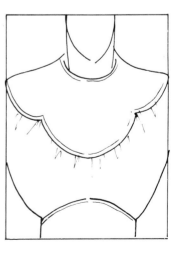

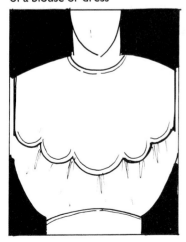

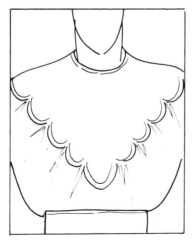

257

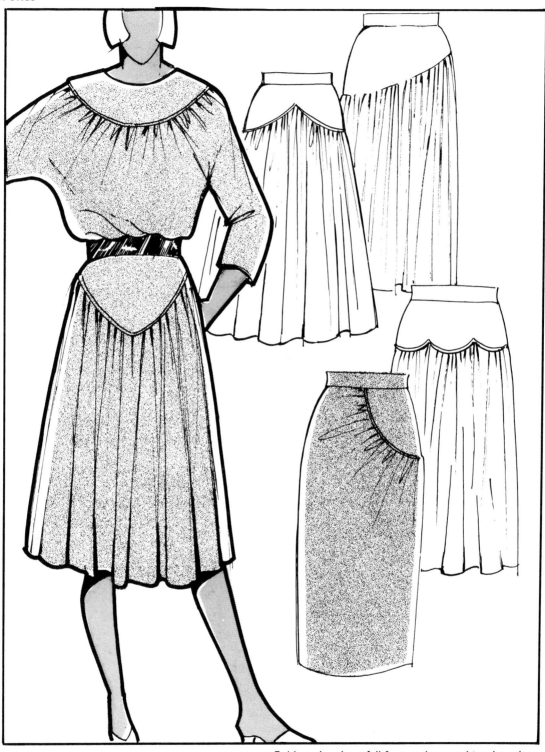

Folds and gathers full from yokes on skirts based on
the curve, emphasising the shape with piping

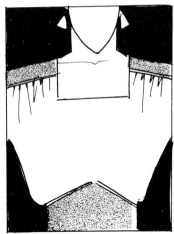

Yokes and gathers

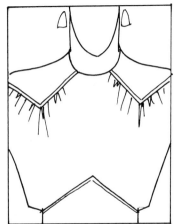

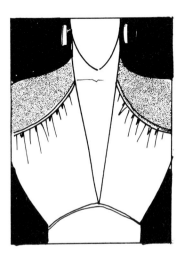

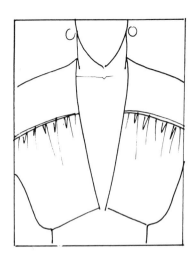

Zips

Zips are made in different widths and lengths. The materials used vary between metal and nylon. The zip, apart from its function as a fastner, has become a fashion detail used on many designs as a decorative fashion feature

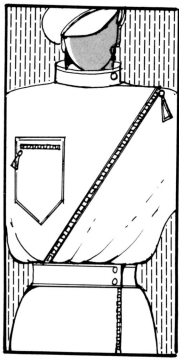

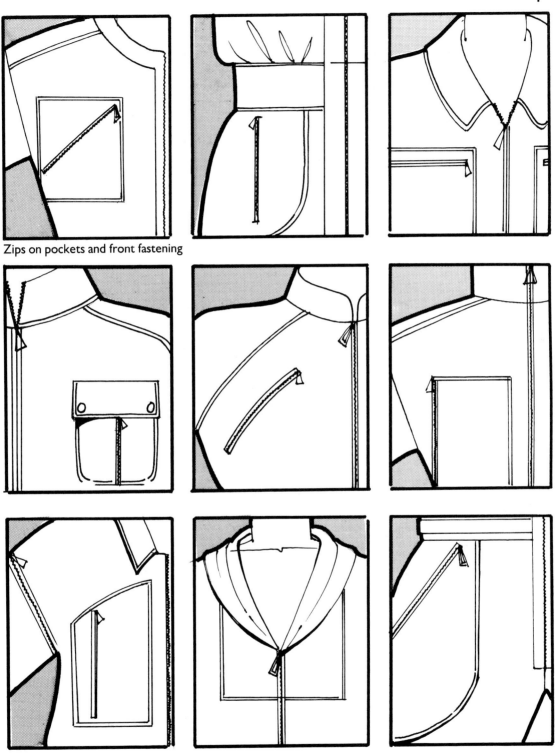

Zips on pockets and front fastening

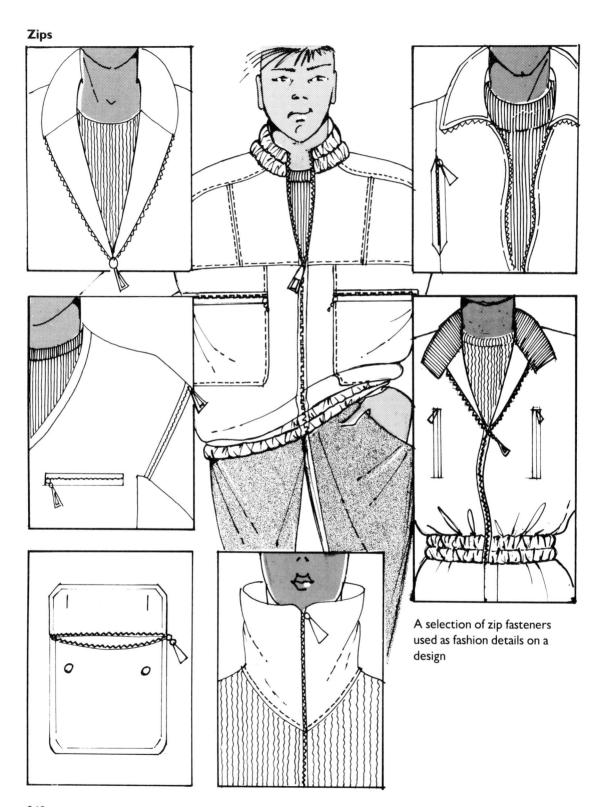

A selection of zip fasteners used as fashion details on a design

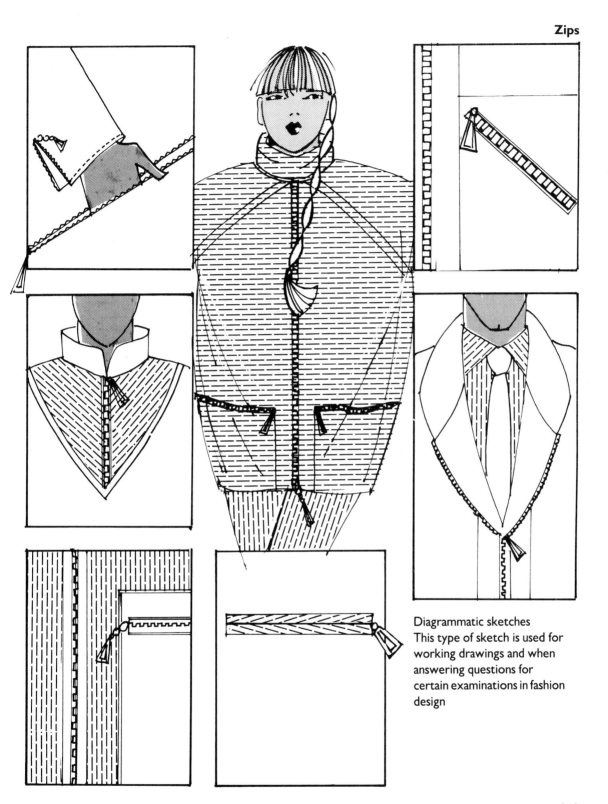

Diagrammatic sketches
This type of sketch is used for working drawings and when answering questions for certain examinations in fashion design

Further reading

Fashion drawing

Ireland, Patrick John, *Fashion Design Drawing and Presentation*, Batsford, 1982

Ireland, Patrick John, *Fashion Design*, Cambridge University Press, 1983

Ireland, Patrick John, *Fashion Drawing*, Cambridge 1986

Ireland, Patrick John, *Introduction to Fashion Design*, Batsford, 1992

Figure drawing and anatomy

Barcsay, Jeno, *Anatomy for the Artist*, Octopus, 1979

Davy, Don, *Anatomy and Life Drawing*, Batsford, 1975

Gordon, Louise, *Anatomy and Figure Drawing*, Batsford paperback, 1985

Kramer, Jack, *Human Anatomy and Figure Drawing*, Van Nostrand Reinhold, 1978

Pattern cutting

Davis, R.I., *Men's Garments 1830-1900: A Guide to Pattern Cutting*, Batsford, 1989

Hamilton Hill, M. and Bucknell, P.A., *The Evolution of Fashion: Pattern and Cut from 1066 to 1930*, Batsford, 1967, 1987

Stanley, Helen, *Modelling and Flat Cutting for Fashion*, 3 volumes, Hutchinson, 1982

Needlework

Butler, Anne, *Batsford Encyclopaedia of Embroidery Stitches*, Batsford paperback, 1983

Ladbury, Ann, *Batsford Book of Sewing*, Batsford, 1979

Reader's Digest Complete Guide to Sewing, Reader's Digest

Vogue Sewing Book, Vogue

Costume research

Ewing, Elizabeth, *History of Twentieth Century Fashion*, Batsford, 1974, 1986, 1992

Fashions of a Decade series, (1920s-90s), Batsford, 1990, 1991

Glynn, Prudence, with Gibsbury, Madeleine, *In Fashion: Dress in the Twentieth Century*, Allen and Unwin, 1978

Gorsline, Douglas, *A History of Fashion*, Batsford, 1991

Peacock, John, *Fashion Sketchbook 1920-1960*, Thames & Hudson, 1977

Ribeiro, Aileen and Cumming, Valerie, *The Visual History of Costume*, Batsford, 1989

Robinson, Julian, *The Golden Age of Style*, Orbis, 1983

Yarwood, Doreen, *The Encyclopaedia of World Costume*, Batsford, 1978

Yarwood, Doreen, *Fashion in the Western World*, Batsford, 1992